Express Web Development

Build Modern Backends with Node.js

Robert Caledhel

Table of Contents

Chapter 1: Welcome to the Server-Side

You've likely spent some time crafting web pages with HTML, styling them with CSS, and maybe even adding interactive elements using JavaScript directly within the browser. That's the *client-side* – what the user sees and interacts with. But where does the data come from? How are user accounts managed? How does a website "remember" you? That's where the *server-side* comes in. Traditionally, server-side development involved languages like PHP, Python, Ruby, or Java. But what if you could use the JavaScript skills you might already have, or are learning, to build the *entire* web application, from the user interface right down to the database interaction? That's the promise of Node.js, and it's completely changed the landscape of web development. In this book, we'll journey through building dynamic, powerful web applications using Node.js and its most popular web framework, Express. Get ready to take JavaScript beyond the browser!

What is Node.js?

Imagine JavaScript stepping out of the confines of the web browser and onto the computer's main operating system. That's essentially what Node.js allows. It's not a programming language itself; rather, it's a **runtime environment** that lets you execute JavaScript code directly on your server, your laptop, or pretty much anywhere you can run code.

JavaScript Everywhere

For years, JavaScript was primarily associated with making web pages dynamic – validating forms, creating animations, fetching data without reloading the page (AJAX). Node.js, created by Ryan Dahl in 2009, broke that mold. It took Google's incredibly fast V8 JavaScript engine, the same one powering browsers like Chrome and Edge, and combined it with libraries that allow JavaScript to interact with the computer's file

1

system, network connections, and operating system features – things browser JavaScript is usually restricted from doing for security reasons. This means you can use JavaScript to write command-line tools, build web servers, interact with databases, and much more.

The V8 Engine

At the heart of Node.js is the V8 engine. Think of V8 as a high-performance translator. It takes your human-readable JavaScript code and converts it into the low-level machine code that the computer's processor can understand and execute very quickly. V8 is constantly being optimized by Google, and Node.js benefits directly from these improvements, making JavaScript a surprisingly performant choice for server-side tasks.

Event-Driven, Non-Blocking I/O

This sounds technical, but it's the secret sauce behind Node.js's efficiency, especially for web applications. Let's break it down with an analogy.

Imagine a restaurant.

- **Blocking Waiter (Traditional Approach):** A waiter takes your order, walks it to the kitchen, *waits* for the chef to cook it, picks up the food, and *then* brings it back to your table. While waiting for the kitchen, the waiter isn't taking orders from other tables or delivering drinks. They are "blocked." If the kitchen is slow, many customers wait, even if they just wanted a glass of water. Many traditional server-side technologies worked somewhat like this, dedicating a whole process or thread to handle one request, waiting for operations like database queries or file reads to complete before doing anything else.

- **Non-Blocking Waiter (Node.js Approach):** A Node.js-style waiter takes your order and immediately gives it to the kitchen. They don't wait. Instead, they instantly move on to take the next table's order, deliver drinks, or clear plates. When the kitchen finishes your dish (an "event"), they signal the waiter, who then efficiently picks it up and delivers it.

Node.js works similarly using an **event loop**. When your code needs to perform an operation that takes time, like reading a file from disk, querying a database, or handling a network request (these are Input/Output or I/O operations), Node.js *doesn't wait*. It delegates that task to the operating system and registers a callback function (a function to run later). It then immediately moves on to handle other incoming requests or tasks. When the slow operation (like reading the file) is complete, the operating sys-

2

tem notifies Node.js, which puts the corresponding callback function onto a queue. The event loop constantly checks this queue; when it's free, it picks up the next completed task's callback and executes it.

This "non-blocking" approach makes Node.js extremely efficient at handling many simultaneous connections, which is typical for web servers. It uses resources much more effectively than waiting around.

Why Choose Node.js?

Beyond its technical underpinnings, several practical reasons make Node.js a compelling choice for web development:

- **Performance:** While not always the absolute fastest for CPU-intensive tasks (like complex calculations), Node.js shines in applications with lots of I/O operations (like web servers handling many user requests, talking to databases, or acting as an API gateway). Its non-blocking nature means it can handle high concurrency with relatively low resource usage.
- **The npm Ecosystem:** Node.js comes with **npm** (Node Package Manager). Think of npm as a colossal, free library of pre-written code modules (packages) for nearly anything you can imagine. Need to work with dates? There's a package. Need to connect to a specific database? There's a package. Need tools for testing, security, or image manipulation? There are packages! This vast ecosystem drastically speeds up development, as you don't have to reinvent the wheel constantly. We'll be using npm extensively throughout this book, starting with installing Express itself.
- **Unified Language:** Perhaps one of the biggest draws, especially for front-end developers, is the ability to use JavaScript for both the client-side (browser) and server-side (Node.js) code. This reduces the context switching required when working with different languages and allows teams to share code and knowledge more easily, leading to potentially faster development cycles.

Setting Up Your Environment

Alright, enough talk! Let's get Node.js installed so you can start running JavaScript on your machine outside the browser.

Installing Node.js and npm

The best way to install Node.js is usually by using the official installers or a version manager.

1. **Go to the Official Website:** Open your web browser and navigate to https://nodejs.org/.
2. **Download the Installer:** You'll typically see two versions offered:
    - **LTS (Long Term Support):** This is the recommended version for most users, especially for production applications. It focuses on stability and security and receives updates for a longer period. **Choose this one**.
    - **Current:** This version has the latest features but might be less stable and changes more frequently. It's great for experimenting with cutting-edge additions but generally not advised for starting production work.
3. **Run the Installer:** Download the installer appropriate for your operating system (Windows, macOS, Linux) and follow the on-screen instructions. The installer will install both Node.js and npm.

(Alternatively, advanced users might prefer using a version manager like nvm *(Node Version Manager) for Linux/macOS or* nvm-windows *for Windows. These tools allow you to easily install and switch between multiple Node.js versions, which can be helpful for working on different projects with different requirements. However, for starting, the direct installer is perfectly fine.)*

Verifying Your Installation

Once the installation is complete, you need to verify that it worked correctly. Open your terminal or command prompt:

- On **Windows:** Search for "Command Prompt" or "PowerShell".
- On **macOS:** Open the "Terminal" app (usually found in Applications > Utilities).
- On **Linux:** Open your distribution's terminal application.

Now, type the following commands, pressing Enter after each one:

```
node -v
```

You should see a version number printed, like v18.17.1 or similar (the exact version will depend on the LTS version available when you installed). This confirms Node.js is installed.

```
# Expected output (version number will vary):
v18.17.1
```

Next, check npm:

```
npm -v
```

You should see another version number, like `9.6.7`. This confirms npm is also installed.

```
# Expected output (version number will vary):
9.6.7
```

If you get "command not found" errors, the installation might not have completed correctly, or the installer didn't add Node.js to your system's PATH environment variable. Double-check the installation steps or consult the Node.js documentation for troubleshooting.

Your First Node Script

Let's write and run a very simple Node.js program.

1. **Create a file:** Open a plain text editor (like VS Code, Sublime Text, Notepad++, or even basic Notepad/TextEdit) and create a new file.

2. **Write the code:** Type the following line of JavaScript into the file:

   ```
   console.log("Hello from Node.js!");
   ```

3. **Save the file:** Save the file with a `.js` extension, for example, `hello.js`, in a location you can easily navigate to in your terminal (like your Desktop or a dedicated project folder).

4. **Run the script:** Open your terminal again and navigate to the directory where you saved `hello.js`. You can use the `cd` (change directory) command. For example, if you saved it on your Desktop:

   - macOS/Linux: `cd ~/Desktop`
   - Windows: `cd Desktop` (or the full path)

   Once you are in the correct directory, run the script using the `node` command followed by the filename:

   ```
   node hello.js
   ```

5. **See the output:** You should see the text "Hello from Node.js!" printed directly in your terminal.

```
# Expected output:
Hello from Node.js!
```

Congratulations! You've successfully executed JavaScript outside of a web browser using Node.js.

Node's Built-in Modules

Node.js comes with a set of essential built-in modules that provide core functionality without needing to install anything extra via npm. Think of these as the standard toolkit that comes with Node.js. You access these modules using the `require` function, which is part of the **CommonJS module system** that Node.js traditionally uses.

Understanding CommonJS Modules

Imagine you're building something complex, like a robot. You wouldn't build every single gear, wire, and sensor from scratch. You'd likely use pre-built components: motors, sensors, a chassis. Modules in Node.js are like these components. They encapsulate related code and functionality into reusable units.

- `require('module-name')`: This is how you bring a module's functionality into your current file. You assign the result to a variable to use the module's features.
- `module.exports`: This is a special object within a file. Anything you assign to `module.exports` (or properties you add to it) becomes available to other files that `require` this file. This is how you create your *own* reusable modules. (We'll explore creating custom modules more later).

Let's look at a couple of important built-in modules:

- `fs` **(File System):** This module provides functions for interacting with the computer's file system – reading files, writing files, creating directories, etc.

```
// Import the built-in 'fs' module
const fs = require('fs');

// Example: Read the content of 'hello.js' synchronously
// (Synchronous is simpler for a quick example, but usually
// asynchronous methods are preferred in Node.js apps!)
```

6

```
try {
  const data = fs.readFileSync('hello.js', 'utf8');
  console.log("Content of hello.js:");
  console.log(data);
} catch (err) {
  console.error("Error reading file:", err);
}
```

(Note: Using synchronous functions like `readFileSync` *can block the event loop. We'll heavily favor asynchronous methods later!)*

- http: This module is fundamental for networking, specifically for creating HTTP servers and clients. It's the low-level foundation upon which frameworks like Express are built.

```
// Import the built-in 'http' module
const http = require('http');

// We won't build a full server here, but know that 'http'
// is the tool for creating servers, handling requests,
// and sending responses in plain Node.js.
// We'll use this directly in the next chapter!
```

- path: This utility module helps you work with file and directory paths in a way that's compatible across different operating systems (Windows uses backslashes \, while macOS/Linux use forward slashes /).

```
// Import the built-in 'path' module
const path = require('path');

const myFile = 'hello.js';
const fullPath = path.join(__dirname, 'subfolder', myFile);

// __dirname gives the directory of the current module
console.log("Constructed path:", fullPath);
// Output will adapt based on your OS (e.g., using \ or /)
```

These are just a few examples. Node.js has many other built-in modules for cryptography, handling streams of data, interacting with the operating system, and more. You can find the full list in the official Node.js documentation.

Chapter Summary

In this chapter, you took your first steps into the server-side world with JavaScript. You learned that Node.js is a runtime environment built on the fast V8 engine, allowing you to run JavaScript anywhere. We explored its efficient event-driven, non-blocking I/O model using the helpful analogy of a responsive waiter. You discovered compelling reasons to use Node.js, including performance benefits, the vast npm ecosystem, and the advantage of using a single language for full-stack development. Most importantly, you set up your development environment by installing Node.js and npm and ran your very first server-side JavaScript code! Finally, you got a glimpse of Node's built-in modules like `fs`, `http`, and `path`, and understood the basic concept of `require` for bringing in functionality.

Now that you have Node.js set up and understand some basic concepts, you're ready to build something more interesting than just printing to the console. In the next chapter, we'll dive deeper into the built-in `http` module and construct your very first simple web server entirely with Node.js, directly handling requests and sending responses. This will give you a solid appreciation for what's happening under the hood before we introduce the Express framework to make things much easier!

Chapter 2: Your First Node.js Web Server

In the last chapter, we set up our Node.js environment and got a feel for running JavaScript outside the browser. We even peeked at some built-in modules like `fs` and `http`. Now, it's time to put that `http` module to work! We're going to build a fundamental piece of the web: a simple web server. This server will listen for incoming requests from browsers and send back responses. Doing this manually, using *only* Node.js's core features, is incredibly insightful. It helps you understand the basic mechanics of web communication and truly appreciate the convenience and power that frameworks like Express (which we'll introduce in Chapter 3) bring to the table. Let's dive into the world of HTTP requests and responses!

Understanding HTTP Basics

Before we write server code, let's quickly recap how web browsers (clients) and web servers talk to each other. They use a protocol called **HTTP (HyperText Transfer Protocol)**, or its secure version, **HTTPS**. Think of it as the language of the web.

At its core, it's a conversation based on **Requests** and **Responses**:

1. **Request:** Your browser (the client) sends an HTTP request to a specific server address (URL) when you type a web address, click a link, or submit a form. This request contains information like:

    - **URL (Uniform Resource Locator):** The address of the resource being requested (e.g., `/about`, `/products/cool-widget`). This includes the path and potentially a **query string** (e.g., `/search?term=node`) for sending extra parameters.
    - **Method:** The action the client wants to perform. Common methods include:
        - `GET`: Retrieve data (e.g., get a web page, get user data).

- POST: Submit data to be processed (e.g., create a new user, submit a form).
  - PUT: Update an existing resource completely.
  - DELETE: Remove a resource.
  - PATCH: Partially update an existing resource.
- **Headers:** Additional information about the request (e.g., what types of responses the browser accepts (Accept), information about the browser itself (User-Agent), data being sent (Content-Type)).

2. **Response:** The server receives the request, processes it, and sends back an HTTP response. This response contains:

   - **Status Code:** A three-digit number indicating the result of the request. You've probably seen 404 Not Found. Other common ones include:
     - 200 OK: The request was successful.
     - 201 Created: A new resource was successfully created (often after a POST).
     - 301 Moved Permanently: The requested resource has moved.
     - 400 Bad Request: The server couldn't understand the request (e.g., invalid data).
     - 403 Forbidden: You don't have permission to access the resource.
     - 500 Internal Server Error: Something went wrong on the server.
   - **Headers:** Additional information about the response (e.g., the type of content being sent (Content-Type: text/html), caching instructions).
   - **Body:** The actual content requested (e.g., HTML code, JSON data, an image file). This might be empty for some responses (like a redirect).

Understanding this request-response cycle is crucial for building any web application. Our Node.js server's job is to listen for these requests, figure out what the client wants based on the URL and method, and then craft an appropriate response.

Creating a Server with the http Module

Let's build that server! Create a new file named server.js.

First, we need to bring in Node's built-in http module using require, just like we did with fs and path in Chapter 1.

```
// server.js
```

```
const http = require('http'); // Import the http module
```

The core of the `http` module for creating servers is the `createServer` method. This method takes one argument: a function that will be executed *every time* a new request hits the server. This function itself receives two important arguments:

- req: An object representing the incoming **request**. It contains properties like `req.url`, `req.method`, and `req.headers`.
- res: An object representing the **response** we will send back. We use methods on this object, like `res.writeHead` and `res.end`, to construct our response.

```
// server.js
const http = require('http');

// This function runs for every incoming request
const requestListener = (req, res) => {
  console.log(`Received request for: ${req.url} using method: ${req.method}`);

  // Set the response header: status code 200 (OK), Content-Type text/plain
  res.writeHead(200, { 'Content-Type': 'text/plain' });

  // Send the response body
  res.end('Hello from our simple Node.js server!\n');
};

// Create the server using our request listener function
const server = http.createServer(requestListener);
```

We've defined *what* the server should do when it gets a request (`requestListener`), but it's not actually listening for requests yet. We need to tell it which network port to listen on. Web servers typically listen on standard ports (like 80 for HTTP and 443 for HTTPS), but for development, we'll use a higher port number (above 1024) that doesn't require special permissions. Let's use port 3000.

The `server.listen` method starts the server. It takes the port number and an optional callback function that runs once the server has successfully started listening.

```
// server.js
const http = require('http');
const port = 3000; // Port to listen on

const requestListener = (req, res) => {
  console.log(`Received request for: ${req.url} using method: ${req.method}`);
```

```
    res.writeHead(200, { 'Content-Type': 'text/plain' });
    res.end('Hello from our simple Node.js server!\n');
};

const server = http.createServer(requestListener);

// Start listening on the specified port
server.listen(port, () => {
  console.log(`Server listening on http://localhost:${port}`);
});
```

Now, save `server.js`. Go to your terminal, navigate to the directory where you saved the file, and run it using Node:

```
node server.js
```

You should see the following output in your terminal:

```
# Expected output:
Server listening on http://localhost:3000
```

Your server is running! Open your web browser and navigate to `http://localhost:3000`. You should see the text "Hello from our simple Node.js server!" displayed on the page. Check your terminal – you'll also see the log message: `Received request for: / using method: GET`. You just handled your first web request with Node.js!

To stop the server, go back to your terminal and press `Ctrl + C`.

Let's break down the response part:

- `res.writeHead(200, { 'Content-Type': 'text/plain' });`: This sends the response headers. We set the status code to `200` (OK) and specify the `Content-Type` header. `text/plain` tells the browser to treat the response body as plain text.
- `res.end('Hello ...!\n');`: This sends the actual content (the body) of the response to the browser and signals that the response is complete. You **must** call `res.end()` for every response to finish the communication.

Handling Different URLs (Basic Routing)

Our current server sends the same response no matter what URL path you visit (e.g., `http://localhost:3000/about`, `http://localhost:3000/contact`). That's not very useful! We need **routing** – the process of determining how to respond based on the requested URL path.

We can implement very basic routing by inspecting the `req.url` property inside our `requestListener` function and using conditional logic (`if/else` or `switch`).

Let's modify `server.js`:

```
// server.js
const http = require('http');
const port = 3000;

const requestListener = (req, res) => {
  console.log(`Received request for: ${req.url} using method: ${req.method}`);

  // Basic Routing
  if (req.url === '/') {
    res.writeHead(200, { 'Content-Type': 'text/plain' });
    res.end('Welcome to the Home Page!\n');
  } else if (req.url === '/about') {
    res.writeHead(200, { 'Content-Type': 'text/plain' });
    res.end('This is the About Page.\nLearn about us!\n');
  } else {
    // Handle all other URLs (404 Not Found)
    res.writeHead(404, { 'Content-Type': 'text/plain' });
    res.end('404 Not Found\nSorry, the page you requested does not exist.\n');
  }
};

const server = http.createServer(requestListener);

server.listen(port, () => {
  console.log(`Server listening on http://localhost:${port}`);
});
```

Save the file, stop the previous server (Ctrl + C), and run it again (node server.js).

Now try these URLs in your browser:

- `http://localhost:3000/`: Shows "Welcome to the Home Page!"
- `http://localhost:3000/about`: Shows "This is the About Page..."
- `http://localhost:3000/some/other/path`: Shows "404 Not Found..."

We've created simple routing! The server now responds differently based on the URL path.

Serving Static Files (The Hard Way)

Websites aren't just plain text. They need HTML structure, CSS styling, and client-side JavaScript interactivity. These are typically served as separate files. Let's try serving a basic HTML file.

First, create a simple HTML file named index.html in the *same directory* as your server.js:

```
<!-- index.html -->
<!DOCTYPE html>
<html lang="en">
<head>
  <meta charset="UTF-8">
  <meta name="viewport" content="width=device-width, initial-scale=1.0">
  <title>My Node App</title>
  <style>
    body { font-family: sans-serif; background-color: #eee; }
    h1 { color: #333; }
  </style>
</head>
<body>
  <h1>Hello from HTML!</h1>
  <p>This file was served by our Node.js server.</p>
</body>
</html>
```

Now, we need to modify server.js to read this file and send its content when the user requests the root path (/). We'll use the built-in fs module again, but this time we'll use its **asynchronous** readFile method. This is crucial because reading from the disk can be slow, and we don't want to block the event loop while waiting (remember the non-blocking waiter?).

fs.readFile takes the file path, an optional encoding (use 'utf8' for text files), and a callback function. The callback receives two arguments: err (an error object if something went wrong, otherwise null) and data (the file content if successful).

```
// server.js
const http = require('http');
const fs = require('fs'); // Include the File System module
```

```javascript
const path = require('path'); // Include the Path module
const port = 3000;

const requestListener = (req, res) => {
  console.log(`Received request for: ${req.url} using method: ${req.method}`);

  if (req.url === '/') {
    // Construct the full path to index.html securely
    const filePath = path.join(__dirname, 'index.html');

    // Read the file asynchronously
    fs.readFile(filePath, 'utf8', (err, data) => {
      if (err) {
        // If error (e.g., file not found), send a 500 server error
        console.error("Error reading file:", err);
        res.writeHead(500, { 'Content-Type': 'text/plain' });
        res.end('Internal Server Error\nCould not read index.html.\n');
      } else {
        // If successful, send the HTML content
        res.writeHead(200, { 'Content-Type': 'text/html' }); // Set correct
type!
        res.end(data);
      }
    });

  } else if (req.url === '/about') {
    res.writeHead(200, { 'Content-Type': 'text/plain' });
    res.end('This is the About Page.\nLearn about us!\n');
  } else {
    res.writeHead(404, { 'Content-Type': 'text/plain' });
    res.end('404 Not Found\nSorry, the page you requested does not exist.\n');
  }
};

const server = http.createServer(requestListener);

server.listen(port, () => {
  console.log(`Server listening on http://localhost:${port}`);
});
```

Notice a few key things:

1. We used `path.join(__dirname, 'index.html')` to create a reliable path to
   the file, regardless of the operating system or where you run the node command from. `__dirname` is a Node.js global variable holding the directory path
   of the currently executing script.

2. We used the **asynchronous** `fs.readFile`. The code *after* the `fs.readFile` call (like handling `/about` or 404s) won't execute for the `/` route until the file reading is done and its callback runs.
3. We added error handling inside the callback. If `fs.readFile` fails (e.g., `index.html` doesn't exist), `err` will be an error object, and we send a `500 Internal Server Error` response.
4. Crucially, when sending the HTML file, we set the `Content-Type` header to `text/html`. This tells the browser to render the content as HTML, not plain text.

Run this updated `server.js`. Now when you visit `http://localhost:3000/`, you should see your styled HTML page!

The Limitations of Plain Node.js

We've successfully built a basic web server that can route requests and even serve static HTML files. However, imagine building a real application this way:

- **Complex Routing**: Our `if/else` structure would become incredibly nested and hard to manage with dozens or hundreds of routes. Handling route parameters (like `/users/123`) or different HTTP methods (POST, PUT) for the same URL would add even more complexity.
- **Serving Static Assets**: We only handled `index.html`. What about CSS files, JavaScript files, images? We'd need to add logic to read different file types, figure out their correct `Content-Type` (e.g., `text/css`, `application/javascript`, `image/jpeg`) – often called the MIME type – and potentially set caching headers. This gets tedious fast.
- **Request Body Parsing**: How would we handle data submitted from an HTML form via a POST request? The data arrives in chunks in the request stream. We'd have to manually collect these chunks, parse them based on their encoding (`application/x-www-form-urlencoded` or `application/json`), and handle potential errors.
- **Middleware**: Often, you want certain code to run on *every* request or specific groups of requests (e.g., logging, checking authentication, adding security headers). Implementing this structure cleanly is tricky with just the basic `http` module.
- **Error Handling**: Our error handling is basic. A robust application needs centralized and more sophisticated error handling.

While it's possible to build complex applications using only Node's built-in modules, it requires writing a lot of boilerplate code to handle these common web development tasks. This is exactly why frameworks were invented!

Chapter Summary

In this chapter, you dove headfirst into building a web server using Node.js's fundamental `http` module. You learned about the essential HTTP request-response cycle, including methods, URLs, headers, and status codes. You successfully created a server that listens on a port, handles incoming requests, and sends back responses. We implemented basic routing using `req.url` and conditional logic, and even tackled serving an HTML file using the asynchronous `fs.readFile` method, remembering the importance of setting the correct `Content-Type` header.

Most importantly, by doing this manually, you've likely gained a deep appreciation for the challenges involved: complex routing logic, tedious static file serving, the need for request body parsing, and the lack of a clear structure for middleware or advanced error handling. These limitations perfectly set the stage for our next chapter, where we'll introduce **Express**, the minimal and flexible Node.js web application framework designed to solve these very problems and make building web applications and APIs significantly faster and more organized.

Chapter 3: Express Fundamentals

In the last chapter, we wrestled with Node.js's built-in `http` module to create a web server. While educational, you probably noticed how quickly things could get messy. Handling different URL paths required nested `if/else` statements, serving a simple HTML file involved manually reading the file and setting headers, and we didn't even touch handling form data or organizing reusable logic efficiently. It felt like we were building the plumbing from scratch every time. Thankfully, we don't have to! The Node.js community has created excellent tools to streamline this process, and the most popular, foundational, and widely used is **Express**. Get ready to leave much of that manual plumbing behind and embrace a more elegant way to build web applications in Node.js.

What is Express?

Express.js, or simply Express, is a **web application framework** for Node.js. Think of it as a lightweight layer built on top of Node's `http` module (which you used in Chapter 2). It provides a robust set of features for web and mobile applications without hiding the core Node.js features you might still need.

Its philosophy is often described as **minimalist and unopinionated**.

- **Minimalist:** Express itself provides a thin layer of fundamental web application features. It doesn't impose a lot of structure or force you into a specific way of doing things initially.
- **Unopinionated:** It doesn't dictate which templating engine you should use (like EJS or Handlebars, which we'll see in Chapter 6), how you should structure your application, or what database tools (ORMs/ODMs) you should integrate with. It provides the core routing and middleware functionalities, letting you choose the best tools for the rest of your specific needs.

The two most significant advantages Express offers right out of the box are:

1. **Simplified Routing:** A much cleaner and more powerful way to handle requests based on URL paths and HTTP methods compared to our manual if/else approach.
2. **Middleware Pipeline:** A mechanism to execute functions in sequence during the request-response cycle, perfect for tasks like logging, authentication, data validation, and more. We'll dedicate Chapter 4 entirely to middleware.

By handling much of the boilerplate involved in setting up an HTTP server, Express lets you focus on defining your application's routes and logic.

Setting Up Your First Express App

Let's create a new project and install Express.

1. **Create a Project Directory:** Open your terminal and create a new folder for your project. Navigate into it:

```
mkdir my-express-app
cd my-express-app
```

2. **Initialize npm:** Just like any Node.js project that uses external packages, we need a package.json file. This file keeps track of your project's details and its dependencies (the packages it needs). The quickest way to create one is using npm init -y. The -y flag automatically accepts the default settings.

```
npm init -y
```

This will create a package.json *file in your directory.*

3. **Install Express:** Now, we use npm to install the Express framework. The --save flag (which is the default in newer npm versions, but good practice to include) ensures Express is listed as a dependency in your package.json.

```
npm install express --save
# Or simply: npm install express
```

You'll see npm download and install Express and its own dependencies. A node_modules *folder and possibly a* package-lock.json *file will appear.*

4. **Create Your App File:** Create a new file named `app.js` inside your my-express-app directory. This will be the entry point for our Express application.

Now, let's write the Express equivalent of the "Hello World" server from Chapter 2. Open `app.js` and add the following code:

```
// app.js
const express = require('express'); // Import the Express library
const app = express(); // Create an instance of an Express application
const port = 3000; // Define the port the server will listen on

// Define a simple route for GET requests to the root URL ('/')
app.get('/', (req, res) => {
  res.send('Hello World from Express!'); // Send a response
});

// Start the server and listen on the specified port
app.listen(port, () => {
  console.log(`Express app listening at http://localhost:${port}`);
});
```

Look how much cleaner this is compared to the `http.createServer` code!

- We `require('express')`.
- We create an application instance: `const app = express();`.
- We define a **route handler** for `GET` requests to the root path (/) using `app.-get()`. This function takes the path and a callback function.
- The callback function receives enhanced `req` (request) and `res` (response) objects.
- We use the convenient `res.send()` method to send the response back to the browser.
- Finally, `app.listen()` starts the server, similar to `server.listen()` from the `http` module.

Run this application from your terminal using Node:

```
node app.js
```

You should see:

```
# Expected output:
Express app listening at http://localhost:3000
```

Open your browser to `http://localhost:3000`. You'll see "Hello World from Express!". Much less code, much clearer intent! Stop the server with `Ctrl + C`.

The Express Application Object

The line `const app = express();` is central. It creates the main Express application object, conventionally named app. This object has methods for:

- **Routing:** Defining how the application responds to client requests based on path and HTTP method (e.g., `app.get()`, `app.post()`, `app.put()`, `app.de-lete()`, `app.all()`).
- **Middleware Configuration:** Applying functions that run during the request-response cycle (`app.use()`). More on this in Chapter 4.
- **Template Engine Configuration:** Setting up view engines for rendering dynamic HTML (`app.set()`). We'll cover this in Chapter 6.
- **Starting the Server:** Binding to a port and listening for connections (`app.l-isten()`).

You'll interact with this app object constantly when building Express applications.

Basic Routing with Express

Routing is determining how an application responds to a client request to a particular endpoint, which is defined by a URI (or path) and a specific HTTP request method (GET, POST, etc.).

Express makes defining routes straightforward. The basic structure is:

```
app.METHOD(PATH, HANDLER);
```

- app is the instance of Express.
- METHOD is an HTTP request method in lowercase (e.g., get, post, put, delete).
- PATH is the path on the server (e.g., /, /about, /users).
- HANDLER is the function executed when the route is matched. It typically takes req (request) and res (response) objects as arguments.

Let's add a few more routes to `app.js`:

```
// app.js
const express = require('express');
const app = express();
```

```
const port = 3000;

// Home page route
app.get('/', (req, res) => {
  res.send('Welcome to the Express Home Page!');
});

// About page route
app.get('/about', (req, res) => {
  res.send('This is the About page, powered by Express.');
});

// A simple POST route example (we'll handle data later)
app.post('/submit-data', (req, res) => {
  res.send('Received your POST request!');
});

// Catch-all for undefined routes (basic 404)
// IMPORTANT: This should come AFTER all other routes
app.use((req, res) => {
  res.status(404).send("Sorry, can't find that!");
});


app.listen(port, () => {
  console.log(`Express app listening at http://localhost:${port}`);
});
```

Run node `app.js` again.

- `http://localhost:3000/` -> "Welcome to the Express Home Page!"
- `http://localhost:3000/about` -> "This is the About page..."
- `http://localhost:3000/nonexistent` -> "Sorry, can't find that!" (with a 404 status code).

Note the simple 404 handler using `app.use()`. This is a basic form of middleware (Chapter 4) that catches any request not handled by the routes defined before it. We also used `res.status(404)` to set the correct HTTP status code before sending the response.

Route Parameters

Often, you need to capture dynamic values from the URL path itself. For example, retrieving a specific user by their ID using a URL like `/users/123`. Express lets you define **route parameters** using a colon (`:`) in the path definition.

```
// Add this route definition BEFORE the 404 handler in app.js

app.get('/users/:userId', (req, res) => {
  // Access the captured parameter via req.params
  const userId = req.params.userId;
  res.send(`You requested information for User ID: ${userId}`);
});
```

Restart the server (Ctrl + C, then node app.js). Now navigate to http://localhost:3000/users/123. You should see "You requested information for User ID: 123". Try changing 123 to something else – req.params.userId will contain whatever value is present in that segment of the URL.

Query Strings

Sometimes data is passed in the URL's **query string** (the part after the ?). For example: /search?term=express&limit=10. Express automatically parses the query string into the req.query object.

```
// Add this route definition BEFORE the 404 handler in app.js

app.get('/search', (req, res) => {
  // Access query parameters via req.query
  const searchTerm = req.query.term;
  const limit = req.query.limit || 'No limit specified'; // Provide default

  if (!searchTerm) {
    res.status(400).send('Search term is required (?term=...)');
  } else {
    res.send(`Searching for "${searchTerm}" with limit: ${limit}`);
  }
});
```

Restart the server.

- http://localhost:3000/search?term=routing: Shows "Searching for "routing" with limit: No limit specified"
- http://localhost:3000/search?term=middleware&limit=5: Shows "Searching for "middleware" with limit: 5"
- http://localhost:3000/search: Shows "Search term is required..." with a 400 status code.

Request and Response Objects in Express

As you've seen, the handler functions receive `req` and `res` objects. Express enhances the standard Node.js `http` request and response objects, adding helpful properties and methods.

Request (`req`) Object

The `req` object represents the incoming HTTP request. Some useful properties added by Express include:

- `req.params`: An object containing properties mapped to the named route parameters (like `:userId` above).
- `req.query`: An object containing the parsed query string parameters.
- `req.body`: Contains key-value pairs of data submitted in the request body (e.g., from a form POST). **Important:** By default, `req.body` is `undefined`. You need to use **middleware** (like `express.json()` or `express.urlencoded()`, covered in Chapter 4) to parse the incoming request body first.
- `req.method`: The HTTP method of the request (e.g., 'GET', 'POST').
- `req.path`: The path part of the request URL.
- `req.headers`: An object containing the request headers.
- `req.ip`: The remote IP address of the client.

Response (`res`) Object

The `res` object represents the HTTP response that the Express app sends. Express provides several convenient methods to send responses, making your life easier than using `res.writeHead()` and `res.end()` manually:

- `res.send([body])`: Sends the HTTP response. It can send strings, Buffer objects, JSON objects, or arrays. Express automatically sets the `Content-Type` header based on the data type (e.g., `text/html` for strings, `application/json` for objects/arrays). It also handles details like setting the `ETag` header.
- `res.json([body])`: Sends a JSON response. It explicitly sets the `Content-Type` to `application/json`. Useful for building APIs (Chapter 10).
- `res.status(code)`: Sets the HTTP status code for the response (e.g., `res.status(404)`). It returns the `res` object, so you can chain it with other response methods like `res.status(404).send('Not Found')`.
- `res.sendStatus(code)`: Sets the status code and sends the corresponding status message (e.g., 'Not Found') as the response body.

- `res.sendFile(path, [options], [callback])`: Transfers the file at the given path. It automatically sets the `Content-Type` header based on the file extension. This is *much* simpler than our manual `fs.readFile` approach in Chapter 2! You typically need Node's built-in `path` module to construct the file path correctly.

Let's add a route to serve the `index.html` file we created in Chapter 2, but using `res.sendFile()`:

```
// app.js
const express = require('express');
const path = require('path'); // <<<< Add Node's path module
const app = express();
const port = 3000;

// Home page route - now serves the HTML file
app.get('/', (req, res) => {
  // Construct the absolute path to the file
  const filePath = path.join(__dirname, '../chapter2/index.html'); // Adjust
path if needed!
  res.sendFile(filePath);
});

// About page route
app.get('/about', (req, res) => {
  res.send('This is the About page, powered by Express.');
});

// ... (other routes: /users/:userId, /search, /submit-data) ...

// Route sending JSON data
app.get('/api/info', (req, res) => {
  res.json({ version: '1.0', framework: 'Express' });
});


// Catch-all 404 handler
app.use((req, res) => {
  res.status(404).send("Sorry, can't find that!");
});


app.listen(port, () => {
  console.log(`Express app listening at http://localhost:${port}`);
});
```

Important: Make sure the path in `path.join(__dirname, '../chapter2/index.html')` correctly points to the `index.html` file you created in the previous chapter's directory relative to where your `app.js` is.

Restart the server.

- `http://localhost:3000/`: Now serves the actual `index.html` file correctly rendered by the browser. Much easier!
- `http://localhost:3000/api/info`: Shows the JSON response `{"version":"1.0","framework":"Express"}`.

Chapter Summary

In this chapter, you transitioned from the manual labor of Node's `http` module to the streamlined world of Express.js. You learned that Express is a minimal and unopinionated web framework that simplifies server creation, routing, and response handling. You set up your first Express project, installed the framework using npm, and wrote a basic "Hello World" application, appreciating its conciseness compared to the plain Node.js approach from Chapter 2.

We explored the fundamentals of Express routing, defining handlers for different HTTP methods and URL paths using `app.get()`, `app.post()`, etc. You learned how to capture dynamic data using route parameters (`req.params`) and query strings (`req.query`). We also looked at the enhanced request (`req`) and response (`res`) objects provided by Express, highlighting convenient methods like `res.send()`, `res.json()`, `res.status()`, and the much simpler `res.sendFile()`.

You've now got the basic building blocks for defining *what* your application should do for different requests. However, many applications need to perform common tasks across multiple routes – like logging requests, parsing incoming data, checking user permissions, or adding security headers. Doing this inside every single route handler would be repetitive and inefficient. This is where Express's powerful middleware system comes in. In the next chapter, we'll unravel the magic of middleware and see how it allows us to create clean, modular, and reusable application logic.

Chapter 4: Middleware Magic

In Chapter 3, we saw how Express dramatically simplifies routing and handling responses compared to plain Node.js. We created different routes using `app.get()` and `app.post()`, accessed route parameters and query strings, and used handy response methods like `res.send()` and `res.sendFile()`. But think about common tasks: logging every request, checking if a user is logged in before accessing certain pages, parsing incoming data from forms, or adding standard security headers. Do we really want to copy and paste that logic into *every single* route handler? Absolutely not! That would be incredibly repetitive and hard to maintain.

This is where Express's most powerful and defining feature comes into play: **middleware**. Middleware functions are the building blocks you'll use constantly to structure your Express applications cleanly and efficiently. Think of your incoming requests traveling down an assembly line. Before reaching the final destination (your specific route handler), they pass through various stations (middleware) that can inspect, modify, or even divert the request. Let's unlock the magic of middleware!

Understanding Middleware

At its core, middleware in Express is simply a **function** that has access to three important objects:

1. The **request object** (`req`)
2. The **response object** (`res`)
3. The `next` **function** in the application's request-response cycle.

These functions can perform a wide variety of tasks:

- Execute any code.
- Make changes to the request and response objects (e.g., add properties to `req`).

- End the request-response cycle (by sending a response using `res.send()`, `res.json()`, etc.).
- Call the *next* middleware function in the stack.

The `next()` Function

The `next()` function is the crucial link in the middleware chain. When a middleware function finishes its work and wants to pass control to the *next* function waiting in line (which could be another middleware function or the final route handler), it **must** call `next()`.

If a middleware function *doesn't* call `next()` and also *doesn't* send a response (like `res.send()`), the request will simply hang – the browser will keep waiting indefinitely because the server never finished processing the request.

So, the typical flow looks like this:

1. A request comes into your Express app.
2. Express passes it to the first middleware function registered.
3. Middleware 1 does its thing (e.g., logs the request). It then calls `next()`.
4. Control passes to Middleware 2.
5. Middleware 2 does its thing (e.g., parses incoming data, adds it to `req.body`). It then calls `next()`.
6. Control passes to the specific route handler (e.g., the function you defined in `app.get('/users/:userId', ...)`) that matches the request's method and path.
7. The route handler processes the request (possibly using data added by middleware) and sends a response (e.g., `res.send(...)`). The cycle ends.

If at any point a middleware function decides it needs to end the cycle early (e.g., an authentication middleware finds the user isn't logged in), it can simply send a response (like `res.status(401).send('Unauthorized')`) and *not* call `next()`.

Writing Your Own Middleware

Let's write a couple of simple middleware functions to see how they work. Middleware functions typically have the signature `(req, res, next)`.

Example 1: Simple Logger

Let's create a middleware function that logs the HTTP method and URL path of every incoming request to the console.

```
// Simple logger middleware
const requestLogger = (req, res, next) => {
  // Log the request method and path
  console.log(`[${new Date().toISOString()}] ${req.method} ${req.url}`);

  // VERY IMPORTANT: Call next() to pass control to the next middleware/handler
  next();
};
```

This function takes `req`, `res`, and `next`. It performs its logging action using `req.-method` and `req.url`. Then, crucially, it calls `next()` so the request processing can continue.

Example 2: Adding Request Time

Here's another middleware that adds a custom property `requestTime` to the `req` object, noting when the request was received by the server. Downstream middleware or route handlers can then access this property.

```
// Middleware to add a timestamp to the request object
const addRequestTime = (req, res, next) => {
  req.requestTime = Date.now(); // Add a custom property
  console.log(`Timestamp added by middleware: ${req.requestTime}`);
  next(); // Pass control
};
```

Again, it does its work and calls `next()`.

Using Middleware

Now that we've written some middleware, how do we tell Express to actually use it? There are several ways, depending on the scope you need.

Application-Level Middleware

This is the most common way to apply middleware that should run for *every single request* to your application. You use the `app.use()` method.

Important: The **order** in which you define middleware with `app.use()` **matters significantly**. Express executes middleware functions in the sequence they are added.

Let's integrate our custom middleware into our `app.js` from Chapter 3.

```
// app.js
const express = require('express');
const path = require('path');
const app = express();
const port = 3000;

// --- Custom Middleware Definitions ---
const requestLogger = (req, res, next) => {
  console.log(`[${new Date().toISOString()}] ${req.method} ${req.url}`);
  next();
};

const addRequestTime = (req, res, next) => {
  req.requestTime = Date.now();
  console.log(`Timestamp added by middleware: ${req.requestTime}`);
  next();
};

// --- Using Middleware at the Application Level ---
// IMPORTANT: Place these BEFORE your route definitions!
app.use(requestLogger);   // Logger runs first for every request
app.use(addRequestTime);  // Timestamp adder runs second for every request

// --- Routes ---
app.get('/', (req, res) => {
  console.log(`Route handler received request at: ${req.requestTime}`);
  const filePath = path.join(__dirname, '../chapter2/index.html'); // Adjust
path
  res.sendFile(filePath);
});

app.get('/about', (req, res) => {
  console.log(`Route handler received request at: ${req.requestTime}`);
  res.send('This is the About page, powered by Express.');
});

// ... other routes (/users/:userId, /search, /api/info) ...
// Make sure to add the console.log(req.requestTime) to other routes
// if you want to see the timestamp there too.

app.get('/users/:userId', (req, res) => {
  console.log(`Route handler received request at: ${req.requestTime}`);
  const userId = req.params.userId;
  res.send(`You requested information for User ID: ${userId}`);
});

app.get('/search', (req, res) => {
```

```
    console.log(`Route handler received request at: ${req.requestTime}`);
    const searchTerm = req.query.term;
    const limit = req.query.limit || 'No limit specified';

    if (!searchTerm) {
      res.status(400).send('Search term is required (?term=...)');
    } else {
      res.send(`Searching for "${searchTerm}" with limit: ${limit}`);
    }
});

app.get('/api/info', (req, res) => {
    console.log(`Route handler received request at: ${req.requestTime}`);
    res.json({ version: '1.0', framework: 'Express', requestTime:
req.requestTime });
});


// Catch-all 404 handler (must be AFTER all other routes/middleware)
app.use((req, res) => {
  // Note: req.requestTime will be available here too!
  console.log(`404 handler received request at: ${req.requestTime}`);
  res.status(404).send("Sorry, can't find that!");
});

app.listen(port, () => {
  console.log(`Express app listening at http://localhost:${port}`);
});
```

Run node app.js. Now, when you visit http://localhost:3000/ or
http://localhost:3000/about, check your terminal. You'll see output like this for
each request:

```
# Expected output (timestamps will vary):
[2023-10-27T10:30:05.123Z] GET /
Timestamp added by middleware: 1698399005123
Route handler received request at: 1698399005123
[2023-10-27T10:30:10.456Z] GET /about
Timestamp added by middleware: 1698399010456
Route handler received request at: 1698399010456
```

This clearly shows:

1. requestLogger ran first.
2. addRequestTime ran second, adding the property.

3. The route handler ran last and was able to access `req.requestTime`.

If you swapped the order of `app.use(requestLogger)` and `app.use(addRequest-Time)`, the timestamp would be logged *before* the main request log line. Order matters!

You can also mount application-level middleware at a specific path. For example:

```
const adminAuthCheck = (req, res, next) => {
  // Pretend authentication check...
  const isAdmin = false; // Simple example
  if (isAdmin) {
    console.log("Admin check passed!");
    next();
  } else {
    res.status(403).send('Forbidden: Admins only!');
    // We DON'T call next() here, ending the cycle.
  }
};


// This middleware only runs for requests starting with /admin
app.use('/admin', adminAuthCheck);

app.get('/admin/dashboard', (req, res) => {
  res.send('Welcome to the Admin Dashboard!'); // Will only be reached if
adminAuthCheck calls next()
});

app.get('/public-page', (req, res) => {
  res.send('This page is public.'); // adminAuthCheck does NOT run for this
route
});
```

Route-Specific Middleware

Sometimes, you only need a middleware function to run for one specific route or a few specific routes. You can pass the middleware function(s) directly to the routing method (`app.get`, `app.post`, etc.) *before* the final route handler function.

```
// A simple middleware to check for a specific query parameter
const requireApiKey = (req, res, next) => {
  const apiKey = req.query.apiKey;
  if (apiKey && apiKey === 'supersecret') { // Example check
    console.log('API Key validated!');
    next(); // Valid key, proceed
  } else {
    res.status(401).send('Unauthorized: Valid apiKey required.');
```

```
    // Invalid or missing key, end cycle
  }
};

// Apply requireApiKey ONLY to this specific route
app.get('/api/protected-data', requireApiKey, (req, res) => {
  // This handler only runs if requireApiKey called next()
  res.json({ data: 'This is super secret data!', requestTime:
req.requestTime });
});

// This route does NOT have the requireApiKey middleware
app.get('/api/public-data', (req, res) => {
  res.json({ data: 'This is public data.', requestTime: req.requestTime });
});
```

Restart the server.

- `http://localhost:3000/api/public-data`: Works fine.
- `http://localhost:3000/api/protected-data`: Responds with Unauthorized: `Valid apiKey required.` (401 status).
- `http://localhost:3000/api/protected-data?apiKey=wrongkey`: Still unauthorized.
- `http://localhost:3000/api/protected-data?apiKey=supersecret`: Works! Shows the secret data.

You can even pass multiple route-specific middleware functions:

```
app.get('/complex-route', middlewareA, middlewareB, (req, res) => {
  // Final handler
});
```

Express will execute `middlewareA`, then `middlewareB`, then the final handler, assuming both middleware functions call `next()`.

Router-Level Middleware

As applications grow, you'll want to group related routes together (e.g., all user-related routes, all product-related routes). Express provides a `Router` object for this purpose. You can apply middleware specifically to an entire router instance using `router-.use()`. This is extremely useful for things like applying authentication checks to all routes within `/admin` or `/api/v1`. We will explore `express.Router` and router-level middleware in detail in **Chapter 5**.

Error-Handling Middleware

What happens when something goes wrong? An error might occur in your synchronous code, or you might detect an error condition in your asynchronous code (like a database lookup failing) and want to trigger a centralized error response. Express has a special type of middleware for this: **error-handling middleware**.

Error-handling middleware functions have a special signature with **four** arguments, instead of three: (err, req, res, next). The presence of that first err parameter tells Express this is an error handler.

```
// Example custom error handling middleware
// IMPORTANT: Define this AFTER all other app.use() and routes!
const customErrorHandler = (err, req, res, next) => {
  console.error('--- ERROR ---');
  console.error(err.stack || err.message); // Log the error stack for debugging

  // Set a generic error status code (or determine based on err type)
  const statusCode = err.status || 500; // Use error status or default to 500

  res.status(statusCode).json({
    error: {
      message: err.message || 'Internal Server Error',
      // Optionally include stack in development, but not production
      stack: process.env.NODE_ENV === 'development' ? err.stack : undefined
    }
  });
  // Note: We don't call next() here for typical error handling,
  // unless we want to pass it to another error handler.
};
```

To use it, you define it using app.use() **after all your other routes and middleware.**

```
// ... (all your other app.use and app.get/post routes) ...

// Example route that might cause an error
app.get('/cause-error', (req, res, next) => {
    // Simulate an error
    try {
        // This could be any synchronous code that throws
        throw new Error("Something broke synchronously!");
    } catch (error) {
        // Pass the error to Express's error handling
        next(error);
    }
});
```

```
app.get('/async-error', async (req, res, next) => {
    try {
        // Simulate an async operation failing
        await someAsyncOperationThatMightFail();
        res.send("Async operation succeeded!");
    } catch (error) {
        console.log("Caught async error, passing to next().");
        // Pass the error from async/await block to Express
        next(error);
    }
});

// Dummy async function for the example
async function someAsyncOperationThatMightFail() {
    return new Promise((resolve, reject) => {
        setTimeout(() => {
            reject(new Error("Async Task Failed!"));
        }, 50);
    });
}

// --- ERROR HANDLING MIDDLEWARE ---
// Define this LAST!
app.use(customErrorHandler);


app.listen(port, () => {
  console.log(`Express app listening at http://localhost:${port}`);
});
```

How it works:

- If you call next() with an argument (e.g., next(someErrorObject)), Express skips all regular middleware and route handlers and jumps directly to the *first* error-handling middleware defined.
- If an error is thrown in synchronous middleware or route handler code, Express catches it and passes it to the error-handling middleware.
- For errors in asynchronous code (like Promise.reject or errors inside async/await blocks), you **must** catch them and explicitly pass them to next(error) for the error handler to be invoked.

Now, if you visit /cause-error or /async-error, instead of crashing or hanging, the request will be handled by customErrorHandler, which will log the error and send a formatted JSON error response with a 500 status code.

Common Built-in and Third-Party Middleware

While writing custom middleware is powerful, many common tasks are handled by middleware included with Express or available as third-party npm packages. You'll use these frequently:

- `express.json()`: Parses incoming request bodies with `Content-Type: application/json`. It makes the parsed JSON data available on `req.body`. Absolutely essential for building APIs that accept JSON data.

  ```
  // Use before routes that need to handle JSON data
  app.use(express.json());

  app.post('/api/items', (req, res) => {
    // req.body will contain the parsed JSON object from the request
    const newItem = req.body;
    console.log('Received item:', newItem);
    // ... (save item to database, etc.) ...
    res.status(201).json({ message: 'Item created', item: newItem });
  });
  ```

- `express.urlencoded({ extended: false })`: Parses incoming request bodies with `Content-Type: application/x-www-form-urlencoded`. This is the default encoding used when submitting standard HTML forms. It makes the parsed form data available on `req.body`.

  - The `extended: false` option uses Node's classic `querystring` library for parsing (simpler, handles basic forms).
  - `extended: true` uses the more powerful qs library, which can handle nested objects and arrays in form data. Choose based on your needs; `false` or `true` are both common.

  ```
  // Use before routes that handle HTML form submissions
  app.use(express.urlencoded({ extended: true })); // Or false

  app.post('/contact-form', (req, res) => {
    // req.body will contain the parsed form data
    const name = req.body.name;
    const email = req.body.email;
    console.log(`Form submission: Name=${name}, Email=${email}`);
    // ... (process form data) ...
    res.send('Thank you for your submission!');
  });
  ```

- `express.static('public')`: Serves static files (like HTML, CSS, client-side JavaScript, images, fonts) from a specified directory. This is Express's way of handling what we did manually with `fs.readFile` in Chapter 2, but much more efficiently and robustly.

  - You typically create a directory named `public` (or `static`, `assets`) in your project root.
  - Place your static files inside this directory (potentially in subfolders like `css`, `js`, `images`).

```
// Serve static files from the 'public' directory
// Place this early, often right after initializing 'app'
app.use(express.static('public'));

// Now, if you have 'public/css/style.css', a request to
// '/css/style.css' will automatically serve that file.
// If you have 'public/index.html', a request to '/' might serve it
// (depending on route order), or '/index.html' will.
// If you have 'public/images/logo.png', request '/images/logo.png'.
```

Any request that matches a file inside the 'public' directory will be handled by this middleware, and it won't proceed to your later routes for that specific request.

- **Brief Mentions:**

  - `morgan`: A popular third-party HTTP request logger middleware. Offers predefined formats (like 'dev', 'combined') or lets you define custom logging formats. Much more flexible than our simple logger. (`npm install morgan`)
  - `cors`: Third-party middleware to enable Cross-Origin Resource Sharing. Essential if your frontend (running on a different domain/port) needs to make requests to your Express API. (`npm install cors`)
  - `helmet`: Third-party middleware that helps secure your Express apps by setting various HTTP headers (like Content Security Policy, X-Frame-Options). We'll look closer at this in Chapter 11 on Security. (`npm install helmet`)

Chapter Summary

Middleware is the backbone of Express application architecture. In this chapter, you learned that middleware functions are simply functions with access to the `req`, `res`, and crucially, the `next` function. They execute sequentially during the request-response cycle, allowing you to perform actions like logging, data parsing, authentication, and validation in a modular and reusable way.

We explored how to write your own middleware and how to apply it at different levels: application-wide (`app.use()`), route-specific (passed directly to `app.METHOD()`), and the special error-handling middleware with its unique four-argument signature (`(err, req, res, next)`). You learned the critical importance of calling `next()` to pass control, or sending a response to end the cycle, and how middleware execution order matters. Finally, we covered essential built-in middleware like `express.json()`, `express.urlencoded()`, and `express.static()`, which handle common tasks like parsing request bodies and serving static files, saving you from writing that boilerplate code yourself.

With a solid understanding of routing (Chapter 3) and middleware (this chapter), you have the core tools to handle requests and structure application logic. However, as applications grow, putting all routes and their handlers in a single `app.js` file becomes unmanageable. In the next chapter, we'll introduce `express.Router` to help us organize our routes into modular, mountable units, leading to cleaner and more scalable project structures.

Chapter 5: Structuring Routes

In the previous chapters, you learned how to define routes using Express (Chapter 3) and how to apply middleware to handle various tasks across requests (Chapter 4). Our `app.js` file started simple, but as we added routes for different pages (`/`, `/about`), API endpoints (`/api/info`), and dynamic paths (`/users/:userId`), you might imagine it getting quite long and crowded in a real application. Having dozens, or even hundreds, of route definitions and their associated handler functions all crammed into one file quickly becomes difficult to read, navigate, and maintain, especially if you're working on a team. We need a way to break our routes down into smaller, more manageable pieces. Thankfully, Express provides an elegant solution for this exact problem: the `express.Router`. Let's organize our growing application!

The Need for Route Organization

Think about building a house. You wouldn't just dump all the materials – wood, pipes, wires, drywall – into one giant pile in the middle of the foundation. You'd organize them. The electrical supplies go together, the plumbing components have their place, and the structural elements are kept separate until needed.

Similarly, in a web application, routes often fall into logical groups:

- Routes related to user authentication (`/login`, `/register`, `/logout`).
- Routes for managing user profiles (`/users`, `/users/:id`, `/users/:id/edit`).
- Routes for handling products in an e-commerce site (`/products`, `/products/:productId`, `/products/category/:categoryName`).
- Routes for administrative tasks (`/admin/dashboard`, `/admin/users`, `/admin/settings`).

Keeping all these diverse routes in a single `app.js` leads to several problems:

- **Readability:** The file becomes excessively long and hard to scroll through to find a specific route.
- **Maintainability:** Modifying or debugging routes for one feature (e.g., products) risks accidentally affecting unrelated routes (e.g., users).
- **Collaboration:** If multiple developers are working on different features, they might constantly run into conflicts trying to edit the same large `app.js` file.

We need a way to group related routes into separate modules, keeping our main `app.js` file clean and focused on configuring the application and bringing these modules together.

Introducing `express.Router`

Express provides a special object called `express.Router` that acts like a "mini-app". You can think of it as a self-contained package of routes and middleware. Instead of defining routes directly on the main `app` object, you define them on an instance of `express.Router`.

Here's how it works:

1. **Create a Router Instance:** You require Express and then call `express.Router()`.
2. **Define Routes:** You use methods like `router.get()`, `router.post()`, `router.use()` (for router-specific middleware) on this router instance, just like you did with the app object.
3. **Export the Router:** You use Node's `module.exports` system (which we briefly saw in Chapter 1) to make your configured router available to other parts of your application.

Let's create a dedicated file for our user-related routes. First, create a new directory named `routes` in your project's root folder (`my-express-app`). Inside this `routes` directory, create a file named `users.js`.

```
// routes/users.js

const express = require('express');
const router = express.Router(); // Create a new router instance

// Define routes on the router instance

// GET request for all users (relative path is '/')
router.get('/', (req, res) => {
```

```
    res.send('List of all users');
    // In a real app, you'd fetch users from a database here
});

// GET request for a specific user by ID
// (relative path is '/:userId')
router.get('/:userId', (req, res) => {
    const userId = req.params.userId;
    res.send(`Details for User ID: ${userId}`);
    // Fetch specific user data here
});

// POST request to create a new user (relative path is '/')
router.post('/', (req, res) => {
    // We'll need body parsing middleware (Chapter 4) enabled in app.js
    const newUserInfo = req.body; // Assumes express.json() or urlencoded is used
    console.log('Creating user with data:', newUserInfo);
    res.status(201).send(`User created successfully!`);
    // Save user to database here
});

// Export the router so it can be used in app.js
module.exports = router;
```

Notice that the paths defined within `routes/users.js` (like `/` and `/:userId`) are relative. They don't know or care yet about the full URL path they will eventually live under in the main application. We've bundled all our user-related route logic into this single, focused module.

Mounting the Router

Now that we have our `users.js` router module, how do we connect it to our main application in `app.js`? We use `app.use()`, but this time, we provide a **path prefix** as the first argument. This tells Express that any request whose path *starts* with this prefix should be handed off to the router module we provide as the second argument. This process is called **mounting** the router.

Let's refactor our `app.js`:

```
// app.js
const express = require('express');
const path = require('path');
const app = express();
const port = 3000;
```

```javascript
// --- Middleware Definitions & Usage ---
// (requestLogger, addRequestTime - optional now, but good practice)
const requestLogger = (req, res, next) => {
  console.log(`[${new Date().toISOString()}] ${req.method} ${req.url}`);
  next();
};
app.use(requestLogger);

// Body parsing middleware (Essential for POST requests in users.js)
app.use(express.json()); // For parsing application/json
app.use(express.urlencoded({ extended: true })); // For parsing form data

// Static files middleware
app.use(express.static('public')); // Assuming 'public' directory exists

// --- Import Routers ---
const userRouter = require('./routes/users'); // Import the user router

// --- Mount Routers ---
// Any request starting with /users will be handled by userRouter
app.use('/users', userRouter);

// --- Other Main App Routes ---
// (Home page, about page, etc., can stay here or move to their own router)
app.get('/', (req, res) => {
  // Serve an index.html or render a template
  res.send('Welcome to the Main App Home Page!');
});

app.get('/about', (req, res) => {
  res.send('This is the main About page.');
});

// --- Error Handling Middleware ---
const customErrorHandler = (err, req, res, next) => {
  console.error('--- ERROR ---');
  console.error(err.stack || err.message);
  const statusCode = err.status || 500;
  res.status(statusCode).json({
    error: { message: err.message || 'Internal Server Error' }
  });
};
// Define this LAST!
app.use(customErrorHandler);
```

```
app.listen(port, () => {
  console.log(`Express app listening at http://localhost:${port}`);
});
```

What's happening here?

1. We require('./routes/users') to import the exported router object from our users.js file.
2. We use app.use('/users', userRouter);. This line tells Express:
   - "Watch for requests where the URL path starts with /users."
   - "If a request matches (e.g., /users, /users/123, /users/abc), strip off the /users prefix and pass the rest of the path (/, /:userId, /abc) along with the req and res objects to the userRouter to handle."

Now, restart your server (node app.js).

- Visiting http://localhost:3000/users will execute the router.get('/', ...) handler inside routes/users.js.
- Visiting http://localhost:3000/users/456 will execute the router.get('/:userId', ...) handler inside routes/users.js, and req.-params.userId will be 456.
- Sending a POST request to http://localhost:3000/users (using a tool like Postman or curl, or later an HTML form) will execute the router.post('/', ...) handler inside routes/users.js.

Our app.js is now cleaner – the specifics of handling user routes are encapsulated in routes/users.js.

Router-Level Middleware

Just like you can apply middleware to the entire application using app.use(), you can also apply middleware that runs *only* for the routes defined within a specific router using router.use(). This is perfect for logic that applies only to a particular section of your site.

For example, let's add a simple middleware to our userRouter that runs before every user-related route handler.

```
// routes/users.js

const express = require('express');
```

```
const router = express.Router();

// --- Router-Level Middleware ---
router.use((req, res, next) => {
  // This runs for ALL requests handled by this router (/users/*)
  console.log(`User Router Middleware: Accessing time ${Date.now()}`);
  // Example: You could check user permissions here
  next(); // Pass control to the next middleware or route handler
});

// GET request for all users (relative path is '/')
router.get('/', (req, res) => {
  res.send('List of all users');
});

// GET request for a specific user by ID
router.get('/:userId', (req, res) => {
  const userId = req.params.userId;
  res.send(`Details for User ID: ${userId}`);
});

// POST request to create a new user
router.post('/', (req, res) => {
  const newUserInfo = req.body;
  console.log('Creating user with data:', newUserInfo);
  res.status(201).send(`User created successfully!`);
});

module.exports = router;
```

Restart the server. Now, *any* request to /users or /users/:userId will first trigger the "User Router Middleware" log message before executing the specific route handler. Requests to / or /about (handled directly by app.js) will *not* trigger this user-specific middleware.

Organizing Your Project Structure

Using routers naturally leads to a more organized project structure. A common convention is to have a dedicated routes directory containing different router modules.

A typical structure might look like this:

```
my-express-app/
├── app.js                    # Main application setup, middleware, mounting
routers
```

```
├── package.json
├── package-lock.json
├── node_modules/
├── public/                    # Static files (CSS, JS, images)
│   ├── css/
│   ├── js/
│   └── images/
└── routes/                    # Directory for router modules
    ├── index.js               # Router for main routes (/, /about, etc. - optional)
    ├── users.js               # Router for /users/* routes
    └── products.js            # Router for /products/* routes (example)
```

In this structure, `app.js` would look something like this:

```js
// app.js (Conceptual Example with multiple routers)
const express = require('express');
const app = express();
const port = 3000;
// --- Middleware ---
app.use(express.json());
app.use(express.urlencoded({ extended: true }));
app.use(express.static('public'));
// ... other global middleware

// --- Import Routers ---
const indexRouter = require('./routes/index');
const userRouter = require('./routes/users');
const productRouter = require('./routes/products');

// --- Mount Routers ---
app.use('/', indexRouter); // Handle routes like / and /about
app.use('/users', userRouter); // Handle routes starting with /users
app.use('/products', productRouter); // Handle routes starting with /products

// --- Error Handling ---
// app.use(customErrorHandler);

app.listen(port, /* ... */);
```

This keeps `app.js` focused on configuration and orchestration, while the logic for specific features resides in separate, manageable router files.

Route Controllers

We've successfully separated our routes into modules. But look inside `routes/user-s.js` – the route definitions (`router.get(...)`) are still mixed with the actual logic that handles the request (the callback functions). As these handler functions grow more complex (e.g., interacting with a database, performing validation), even the router files can become cluttered.

A further refinement is to separate the route handler logic into its own set of functions, often called **controllers**. The router file then becomes responsible only for mapping URL paths and HTTP methods to the appropriate controller function. The controller functions contain the actual logic for processing the request and sending a response.

1. **Create a `controllers` directory**: Add a new directory named `controllers` at the project root.
2. **Create controller files**: Inside `controllers`, create files corresponding to your resources (e.g., `userController.js`).
3. **Define handler functions in controllers**: Move the logic from the router callbacks into exported functions within the controller file. These functions still take (`req`, `res`, `next`) as arguments.
4. **Import and use controllers in routers**: Modify the router file to `require` the controller and pass the controller functions as the handlers in the route definitions.

Let's refactor:

Create `controllers/userController.js`:

```
// controllers/userController.js

// Function to handle GET /users
const getAllUsers = (req, res) => {
  console.log('Controller: Fetching all users');
  // Database logic would go here
  res.send('List of all users (from controller)');
};

// Function to handle GET /users/:userId
const getUserById = (req, res) => {
  const userId = req.params.userId;
  console.log(`Controller: Fetching user ${userId}`);
  // Database logic for specific user
```

```
    res.send(`Details for User ID: ${userId} (from controller)`);
};


// Function to handle POST /users
const createUser = (req, res) => {
  const newUserInfo = req.body;
  console.log('Controller: Creating user with data:', newUserInfo);
  // Database logic to save user
  res.status(201).send(`User created successfully! (from controller)`);
};


// Export the controller functions
module.exports = {
  getAllUsers,
  getUserById,
  createUser,
};
```

Modify routes/users.js **to use the controller:**

```
// routes/users.js

const express = require('express');
const router = express.Router();
const userController = require('../controllers/userController'); // Import
controller

// --- Router-Level Middleware (Optional) ---
router.use((req, res, next) => {
  console.log(`User Router Middleware: Accessing time ${Date.now()}`);
  next();
});


// --- Define Routes using Controller Functions ---

// GET request for all users
router.get('/', userController.getAllUsers);

// GET request for a specific user by ID
router.get('/:userId', userController.getUserById);

// POST request to create a new user
router.post('/', userController.createUser);

module.exports = router;
```

Our `routes/users.js` file is now incredibly clean! It purely defines the *structure* of the user-related routes and delegates the actual *work* to the `userController`. This separation of concerns makes the code:

- **More Organized:** Clear distinction between routing definition and business logic.
- **More Reusable:** Controller functions could potentially be called from other parts of the application (though less common for direct route handlers).
- **Easier to Test:** You can test controller functions in isolation, without needing to simulate HTTP requests.

The recommended project structure now looks even better:

```
my-express-app/
├── app.js
├── package.json
├── node_modules/
├── public/
├── routes/
│   ├── index.js
│   ├── users.js          # Maps routes to controllers
│   └── products.js
└── controllers/
    ├── indexController.js
    ├── userController.js # Contains route handler logic
    └── productController.js
```

Chapter Summary

In this chapter, we tackled the challenge of organizing routes in a growing Express application. You learned that keeping all routes in a single `app.js` file leads to poor readability and maintainability. The solution is `express.Router`, which acts like a mini-application, allowing you to group related routes and middleware into separate modules.

We saw how to create router instances, define routes and middleware on them (`router.get`, `router.use`), and export them using `module.exports`. You learned how to **mount** these routers onto specific path prefixes in your main `app.js` file using `app.use('/prefix', router)`. We also explored applying router-level middleware for logic specific to a group of routes.

Finally, we introduced the **controller** pattern as a further refinement. By separating route handler logic into controller functions and keeping router files focused solely on mapping paths to these functions, you achieve a highly organized, testable, and scalable application structure. We established a common project layout with distinct `routes` and `controllers` directories.

With your backend application structure now neat and tidy, you're well-prepared to handle more complex features. Our server can handle requests and route them efficiently, but so far, our responses have been mostly plain text or simple JSON. In the next chapter, we'll explore **Templating Engines**, which allow us to dynamically generate rich HTML responses by combining data from our server with HTML templates, making our web application interfaces much more engaging.

Chapter 6: Templating Engines

So far on our journey with Node.js and Express, we've built servers that can respond with plain text (Chapter 2), structured JSON data (perfect for APIs, as we saw briefly in Chapter 3 and will revisit in Chapter 10), and even serve complete, pre-written static files like `index.html` (using `res.sendFile` in Chapter 3). This is great, but most web applications you use aren't static. They display dynamic content – your username when you log in, a list of products fetched from a database, search results tailored to your query. How do we generate HTML on the server that includes this kind of dynamic information before sending it to the user's browser?

Manually constructing HTML strings inside our route handlers by concatenating bits of data would be incredibly messy and error-prone. Imagine trying to build a complex user profile page that way! This is where **templating engines** come to the rescue. They provide a clean and efficient way to embed dynamic data into static templates, generating the final HTML for the user.

What are Templating Engines?

Think of a templating engine like a sophisticated mail merge tool, but for web pages. You create a template file (usually resembling HTML) that contains placeholders and simple logic. Then, in your Express route handler, you provide data (like a user's name or a list of products) to the templating engine along with the name of the template file. The engine processes the template, replaces the placeholders with the actual data, executes any embedded logic (like loops or conditionals), and produces a final HTML string, which Express then sends back to the browser.

Why use them?

- **Separation of Concerns:** Templating engines help separate the presentation logic (how the data looks, the HTML structure) from the application logic (fetching data, handling requests in your controllers from Chapter 5). Your HTML templates focus on the structure and display, while your JavaScript code focuses on the data and control flow. This makes code easier to understand, modify, and maintain.

- **Readability and Maintainability:** Writing HTML with embedded placeholders is much cleaner and more readable than trying to build HTML strings in JavaScript. Changes to the page structure can be made directly in the template file without digging through complex JavaScript code.
- **Reusability:** Templating engines often allow you to create reusable components or "partials" (like headers, footers, sidebars) that can be included in multiple pages, reducing code duplication.

Popular Choices (EJS, Handlebars, Pug)

The Node.js ecosystem offers various templating engines, each with its own syntax and philosophy. Some popular ones include:

- **Pug (formerly Jade):** Known for its significant whitespace-based syntax, which results in very concise templates by omitting HTML tags entirely. It uses indentation to define structure. While powerful, its syntax can be unfamiliar if you're used to standard HTML.
- **Handlebars:** Uses double curly braces {{ }} for placeholders and helpers. Its syntax is logic-less in the templates themselves (promoting separation of concerns), relying on "helpers" defined in JavaScript for more complex logic. It's widely used and quite powerful.
- **EJS (Embedded JavaScript):** Stands out because it lets you write plain JavaScript directly within your templates using specific tags (<% %>, <%= %>). Its syntax feels very familiar if you already know HTML and JavaScript, making the learning curve relatively gentle.

For this book, we'll primarily use **EJS**. Its direct embedding of JavaScript makes it easy to get started and understand the core concepts of server-side rendering without learning a completely new syntax paradigm immediately. The principles you learn with EJS are transferable to other engines if you choose to explore them later.

Setting up a Template Engine (EJS Example)

Integrating EJS into your Express application is straightforward.

1. **Install EJS:** Use npm to add EJS as a project dependency. Open your terminal in your project directory (my-express-app) and run:

```
npm install ejs --save
# Or: npm install ejs
```

2. **Configure Express:** You need to tell Express two things:

   - Which template engine to use (view engine).
   - Where to find your template files (views directory).

   Add these lines to your app.js file, typically near the top after you create the app instance:

```
// app.js
const express = require('express');
const path = require('path'); // Make sure path is required
const app = express();
const port = 3000;

// --- View Engine Setup ---
app.set('view engine', 'ejs'); // Tell Express to use EJS
// By default, Express looks for views in a directory named "views"
// You can customize it like this if needed:
app.set('views', path.join(__dirname, 'views')); // Use path.join for
reliability

// ... (rest of your middleware: body-parser, static, logger) ...
app.use(express.json());
app.use(express.urlencoded({ extended: true }));
app.use(express.static('public'));
// ...

// ... (routers) ...

// ... (error handling) ...

app.listen(port, /* ... */);
```

   - app.set('view engine', 'ejs'); registers EJS as the default engine.
   - app.set('views', path.join(__dirname, 'views')); tells Express
     to look for template files inside a views folder located in your project's
     root directory (__dirname). Using path.join ensures this works cor-
     rectly across different operating systems.
3. **Create the** views **Directory:** In the root of your project (my-express-app), create a new folder named views. This is where all your .ejs template files will
   live.

Rendering Views

Instead of using `res.send()` or `res.sendFile()`, you now use the `res.render()` method to render a template file and send the resulting HTML to the client.

`res.render()` takes two main arguments:

1. `view`: The name of the view file (inside your `views` directory) **without** the file extension (Express adds `.ejs` automatically because we set the `view` engine).
2. `locals` (optional): An object whose properties are passed as local variables accessible within the template file.

Let's create a simple homepage view. Create a file named `home.ejs` inside the `views` directory:

```
<!-- views/home.ejs -->
<!DOCTYPE html>
<html lang="en">
<head>
  <meta charset="UTF-8">
  <title>My Dynamic App</title>
  <link rel="stylesheet" href="/css/style.css"> <!-- Assuming style.css is in
public/css -->
</head>
<body>
  <h1>Welcome to the Home Page!</h1>
  <p>This page was rendered using EJS.</p>
  <p>The current time is: (We'll add this dynamically soon)</p>
</body>
</html>
```

(Note: Make sure you have a `public/css/style.css` *file if you link to it, or remove the* `<link>` *tag.)*

Now, modify the home route (/) in `app.js` (or preferably, in a dedicated `routes/index.js` and `controllers/indexController.js` if you followed Chapter 5's structure) to use `res.render()`:

```
// In your route handler for GET '/'
// (e.g., inside controllers/indexController.js or directly in
app.js/routes/index.js)

const getHomePage = (req, res) => {
  // Render the 'home.ejs' view file
  // Pass an object with data to the template
```

```
  const viewData = {
    pageTitle: "Dynamic Home", // Example data
    currentTime: new Date().toLocaleTimeString()
  };
  res.render('home', viewData); // Renders views/home.ejs
};

// Make sure this route is defined:
// In app.js: app.get('/', getHomePage);
// Or in routes/index.js: router.get('/', indexController.getHomePage);
```

Restart your server (node app.js). Visit http://localhost:3000/. You should see the HTML content from home.ejs. We passed data (pageTitle, currentTime), but we haven't used it in the template yet!

Template Syntax (EJS Example)

EJS uses specific tags to embed JavaScript and output data within your HTML templates:

- <%= value %> **(Output Escaped):** This is the most common tag. It evaluates the JavaScript value inside it and outputs the result directly into the HTML, but it **escapes** special HTML characters (like <, >, &). This is a crucial security feature to prevent Cross-Site Scripting (XSS) attacks when displaying user-provided data. Always use this tag by default for outputting variables.

- <%- value %> **(Output Unescaped):** This tag outputs the evaluated value **without** escaping HTML characters. Use this with caution! It's primarily needed when you *intentionally* want to render raw HTML, such as when including another template file (partials). **Never use this tag to output data that came directly from a user**, as it could allow them to inject malicious scripts.

- <% script %> **(Scriptlet Tag):** This tag executes the JavaScript script inside it but *does not* output anything directly to the HTML. It's used for control flow logic like if statements, for loops, defining variables within the template, etc.

- <%# comment %> **(Comment Tag):** For server-side comments within your EJS template. These comments are not included in the final HTML output sent to the browser.

Let's update views/home.ejs to use the data we passed:

```
<!-- views/home.ejs -->
<!DOCTYPE html>
<html lang="en">
<head>
  <meta charset="UTF-8">
  <!-- Use the dynamic page title -->
  <title><%= pageTitle %></title>
  <link rel="stylesheet" href="/css/style.css">
</head>
<body>
  <h1>Welcome to the Dynamic Home Page!</h1>
  <p>This page was rendered using EJS.</p>
  <%# This is an EJS comment %>

  <!-- Output the current time using escaping tag -->
  <p>The current server time is: <strong><%= currentTime %></strong></p>

  <% // Use scriptlet tags for logic %>
  <% const userLoggedIn = true; // Simulate user state %>
  <% const items = ['Apple', 'Banana', 'Cherry']; %>

  <% if (userLoggedIn) { %>
    <p>Status: You are logged in!</p>
  <% } else { %>
    <p>Status: Please log in.</p>
  <% } %>

  <h2>Available Items:</h2>
  <% if (items.length > 0) { %>
    <ul>
      <% items.forEach(item => { %>
        <li><%= item %></li> <%# Output each item (escaped) %>
      <% }); %>
    </ul>
  <% } else { %>
    <p>No items available.</p>
  <% } %>

</body>
</html>
```

Restart the server and refresh `http://localhost:3000/`. You'll see the dynamic `page-Title` in the browser tab, the current time displayed, the "logged in" status message, and the list of items rendered using the `forEach` loop! Notice how standard JavaScript syntax works within the `<% %>` tags.

Including Partials

Repeating the same HTML structure (like headers, footers, navigation bars) on every page is inefficient. Templating engines allow you to create reusable chunks of HTML called **partials** (or includes).

1. **Create a `partials` subdirectory:** Inside your `views` directory, create a folder named `partials`.

2. **Create partial files:** Create files like `header.ejs` and `footer.ejs` inside `views/partials`.

```
<!-- views/partials/header.ejs -->
<header>
  <nav>
    <a href="/">Home</a> |
    <a href="/about">About</a>
    <%# Add more links as needed %>
  </nav>
  <hr>
</header>

<!-- views/partials/footer.ejs -->
<footer>
  <hr>
  <p>&copy; <%= new Date().getFullYear() %> My Awesome App</p>
</footer>
```

3. **Include partials in main views:** Use the `<%- include('path/to/partial') %>` tag within your main template files. **Crucially, use the unescaped output tag `<%-` here**, because you want to render the *raw HTML* contained within the partial file, not an escaped version of it. The path is relative to the `views` directory.

Let's update `views/home.ejs` again:

```
<!-- views/home.ejs -->
<!DOCTYPE html>
<html lang="en">
<head>
  <meta charset="UTF-8">
  <title><%= pageTitle %></title>
  <link rel="stylesheet" href="/css/style.css">
</head>
<body>
```

```
<%- include('partials/header') %> <%# Include the header partial %>

<h1>Welcome to the Dynamic Home Page!</h1>
<p>This page was rendered using EJS.</p>

<p>The current server time is: <strong><%= currentTime %></strong></p>

<% const userLoggedIn = true; %>
<% const items = ['Apple', 'Banana', 'Cherry']; %>

<% if (userLoggedIn) { %>
  <p>Status: You are logged in!</p>
<% } else { %>
  <p>Status: Please log in.</p>
<% } %>

<h2>Available Items:</h2>
<% if (items.length > 0) { %>
  <ul>
    <% items.forEach(item => { %>
      <li><%= item %></li>
    <% }); %>
  </ul>
<% } else { %>
  <p>No items available.</p>
<% } %>

<%- include('partials/footer') %> <%# Include the footer partial %>
</body>
</html>
```

Restart the server and refresh. Your home page now includes the header and footer content! You can create other views (like an about.ejs) and include the same header and footer partials, ensuring consistency across your site.

Layouts

While including header and footer partials works well, sometimes you want a more robust "layout" file that defines the main HTML skeleton (<html>, <head>, <body> tags), and your individual page views only need to fill in the specific content sections.

EJS doesn't have a built-in layout system quite like some other engines, but the partial-based approach is very common and effective. You can achieve a layout structure by having your main view files include standard header/footer partials as shown above.

For more complex scenarios, libraries like `express-ejs-layouts` exist, but for most cases, structuring your application with well-defined header, footer, and potentially sidebar partials provides a clear and manageable way to handle shared page elements.

Chapter Summary

In this chapter, you learned how to break free from sending static responses and start generating dynamic HTML using templating engines. We discussed why they are essential for separating presentation from logic and improving maintainability. We focused on EJS due to its familiar JavaScript-like syntax.

You learned how to install EJS (`npm install ejs`), configure it in Express (`app.set('view engine', 'ejs')`), and create template files in the `views` directory. We covered the core EJS syntax: outputting escaped data with `<%= %>` (important for security!), outputting unescaped data (like HTML partials) with `<%- %>`, and executing JavaScript logic with `<% %>`. You saw how to pass data from your Express controllers/ routes to your views using the `locals` object in `res.render('viewName', locals)`. Finally, we implemented reusable page sections using partials included with `<%- include('path/to/partial') %>`, forming a basic layout structure.

Now your application can present dynamic information within well-structured HTML pages. But where does this dynamic information ultimately come from? Hardcoding data like user status or item lists in our templates or controllers isn't sustainable. Real applications need to store and retrieve data persistently. In the next chapter, we'll dive into connecting your Express application to databases, allowing you to manage application data effectively.

Chapter 7: Working with Data - Databases

In the last chapter, we unlocked the ability to generate dynamic HTML pages using templating engines like EJS. We could pass data from our server into templates to display things like the current time or a list of items. But where did that data come from? For our examples, we just hardcoded it directly in our route handlers. That works for simple demonstrations, but real web applications need data that *persists*. What happens when the server restarts? Our hardcoded list of items vanishes! What if multiple users need to add or view data simultaneously? We need a robust way to store, retrieve, update, and manage information reliably. Welcome to the world of **databases**. Connecting your Express application to a database is the crucial next step in building truly functional and dynamic web applications.

Why Databases?

Imagine your application manages user accounts, blog posts, product inventory, or customer orders. You can't just keep this information in temporary variables inside your running Node.js process. Why?

- **Persistence:** Variables in your code only exist as long as the program is running. If the server crashes or restarts (which happens during updates or maintenance), all that data is lost. Databases store data independently of your application process, typically on disk, ensuring it persists even when your application isn't running.
- **Structured Storage:** Databases provide organized ways to store data, making it easier to manage and query. Instead of just a loose collection of information, you have defined structures (like tables or collections) with specific data types.
- **Efficient Querying:** Databases are highly optimized for retrieving specific pieces of data. Need to find all users in a specific city? Or all products under a certain price? Databases provide powerful query languages (like SQL or spe-

cific methods for NoSQL databases) to fetch exactly what you need quickly, without having to manually sift through mountains of unstructured data.

- **Concurrency:** Databases are designed to handle multiple connections and operations happening at the same time (concurrency) safely, preventing data corruption when several users or processes try to read or write data simultaneously.

In short, databases are the dedicated storage layer for your application's important information.

Database Types Overview

There's a wide world of databases out there, but they generally fall into two main categories:

- **Relational Databases (SQL):** These databases have been around for decades and are based on the relational model. Think of data organized into **tables**, where each table has predefined **columns** (with specific data types like text, number, date) and data is stored in **rows** (also called records). Examples include:

  - **PostgreSQL:** A powerful, open-source object-relational database known for its feature set and compliance with SQL standards.
  - **MySQL:** Another extremely popular open-source relational database, widely used in web development (often part of the classic LAMP stack).
  - **SQLite:** A lightweight, file-based relational database. Great for development, testing, or simple applications where you don't need a separate database server process.
  - **Microsoft SQL Server, Oracle Database:** Major commercial relational databases. Relational databases use **SQL (Structured Query Language)** for defining structures and manipulating data (querying, inserting, updating, deleting). They excel at enforcing data consistency through relationships between tables (e.g., ensuring an order always belongs to a valid customer).

- **NoSQL Databases (Not Only SQL):** This is a broader category encompassing various database types that emerged to handle different kinds of data and scaling challenges, often diverging from the strict table structure of relational databases. Common types include:

- **Document Databases (e.g., MongoDB, Couchbase):** Store data in flexible, JSON-like **documents**. Each document can have a different structure. Documents are grouped into **collections**. They are very popular with Node.js due to their natural fit with JavaScript's object notation.
- **Key-Value Stores (e.g., Redis, Memcached):** Simple databases that store data as key-value pairs. Extremely fast for lookups, often used for caching or session management.
- **Column-Family Stores (e.g., Cassandra, HBase):** Optimized for queries over large datasets by storing data in columns rather than rows.
- **Graph Databases (e.g., Neo4j):** Designed specifically for storing and navigating data with complex relationships (like social networks or recommendation engines).

Choosing Between SQL and NoSQL:

- **SQL databases** are generally a good choice when:
  - Your data has a clear, predefined structure that doesn't change frequently.
  - Data integrity and consistency through relationships are paramount (e.g., financial transactions).
  - You need complex querying capabilities involving multiple tables (joins).
- **NoSQL databases** (especially Document databases like MongoDB) are often favored when:
  - Your data structure is evolving or varies significantly between items (schema flexibility).
  - You need high scalability and performance for large amounts of data or high traffic loads (often easier to scale horizontally).
  - Development speed is crucial, and the flexible structure aligns well with object-oriented or JavaScript development.

For this book, we'll focus on using **MongoDB**, a popular NoSQL document database, as it integrates very naturally with Node.js and JavaScript. To make interacting with MongoDB even easier from our Express application, we'll use a library called **Mongoose**.

Connecting to a Database (MongoDB with Mongoose Example)

MongoDB stores data in BSON (Binary JSON) documents, which map very cleanly to JavaScript objects. While you can use the official MongoDB Node.js driver directly, **Mongoose** provides a higher-level abstraction called an **ODM (Object Data Modeling)** library.

Think of Mongoose like this:

- It helps you define a **Schema** for your data (a blueprint for your documents), providing structure within MongoDB's flexible environment.
- It creates **Models** based on those Schemas, giving you a clean, object-oriented way to interact with your MongoDB collections (Create, Read, Update, Delete - CRUD operations).
- It handles data validation based on your Schema definitions.
- It simplifies casting data types and managing database connections.

Let's get Mongoose set up.

1. **Install Mongoose:** Add it to your project using npm:

   ```
   npm install mongoose --save
   # Or: npm install mongoose
   ```

2. **Establish a Connection:** You need to tell Mongoose where your MongoDB database is running. MongoDB uses a connection string URI (Uniform Resource Identifier).

   - **For Local Development:** If you've installed MongoDB locally (see MongoDB's documentation for installation instructions), the default URI is usually `mongodb://localhost:27017/yourDatabaseName`. Replace `yourDatabaseName` with a name for your project's database (e.g., `myExpressAppDB`). Mongoose will create the database if it doesn't exist when you first write data to it.
   - **For Cloud Databases:** If you're using a cloud service like MongoDB Atlas, you'll get a specific connection string from their dashboard, often including username/password credentials.

   It's **critical** not to hardcode database credentials directly in your source code. We'll use environment variables for this. First, install the `dotenv` package, which loads variables from a `.env` file into `process.env`:

```
npm install dotenv --save
# Or: npm install dotenv
```

Now, create a file named .env in the **root** of your project (make sure to add
.env to your .gitignore file to avoid committing sensitive credentials!).

```
# .env file
MONGODB_URI=mongodb://localhost:27017/myExpressAppDB
# Or for a cloud DB with credentials (replace placeholders):
#
MONGODB_URI=mongodb+srv://yourUsername:yourPassword@yourcluster.mongodb.
net/myExpressAppDB?retryWrites=true&w=majority
```

Now, in your main application file (app.js or perhaps a dedicated configuration file like config/db.js), you can load dotenv and connect Mongoose:

```
// app.js (or config/db.js)
const mongoose = require('mongoose');
require('dotenv').config(); // Load environment variables from .env file

const connectDB = async () => {
  try {
    const conn = await mongoose.connect(process.env.MONGODB_URI, {
      // Options to avoid deprecation warnings (check Mongoose docs for
current recommendations)
      useNewUrlParser: true,
      useUnifiedTopology: true,
      // useCreateIndex: true, // No longer needed in Mongoose 6+
      // useFindAndModify: false // No longer needed in Mongoose 6+
    });
    console.log(`MongoDB Connected: ${conn.connection.host}`);
  } catch (error) {
    console.error(`Error connecting to MongoDB: ${error.message}`);
    process.exit(1); // Exit process with failure
  }
};

// Call the function to connect
// If you put this in a separate file, export connectDB and call it in
app.js
connectDB();

// --- Important Note ---
// In a real app, you might structure this differently.
```

```
// You could export the connectDB function and call it once when your
app starts.
// Or establish the connection before starting the Express server.
// For simplicity here, we're connecting directly in app.js.
```

This code does the following:

- Requires `mongoose` and `dotenv`.
- Calls `dotenv.config()` to load the `.env` file variables.
- Defines an `async` function `connectDB`.
- Inside `try`, it attempts to connect using `mongoose.connect()`, passing the URI from `process.env.MONGODB_URI`. The options object helps ensure compatibility.
- If successful, it logs the host it connected to.
- If an error occurs (`catch` block), it logs the error and exits the application, as a database connection is usually essential.
- Finally, it calls `connectDB()` to initiate the connection when the file is run.

Run `node app.js`. You should see the "MongoDB Connected" message if everything is set up correctly.

Defining Schemas and Models

Now that we're connected, we need to tell Mongoose about the structure of the data we want to store.

- **Schema:** A Mongoose Schema defines the structure of the documents within a MongoDB collection. It specifies field names, data types (String, Number, Date, Boolean, Array, ObjectId, etc.), default values, validation rules, and more.
- **Model:** A Mongoose Model is a constructor compiled from a Schema definition. An instance of a model represents a MongoDB document and provides the interface for creating, querying, updating, and deleting documents of that type.

Let's create a simple `Task` schema and model. Create a new directory named `models` in your project root, and inside it, create a file named `Task.js`.

```
// models/Task.js
const mongoose = require('mongoose');
```

```
// Define the schema for a Task
const taskSchema = new mongoose.Schema({
  description: {
    type: String,
    required: [true, 'Task description cannot be empty'], // Basic validation
    trim: true // Remove leading/trailing whitespace
  },
  completed: {
    type: Boolean,
    default: false // Default value if not specified
  },
  createdAt: {
    type: Date,
    default: Date.now // Automatically set creation date
  }
  // You can add more fields like priority (Number), dueDate (Date), etc.
});

// Create the Model based on the Schema
// Mongoose will automatically look for the plural, lowercase version
// of your model name for the collection ('tasks' in this case).
const Task = mongoose.model('Task', taskSchema);

// Export the Model
module.exports = Task;
```

This defines a `Task` with a required `description` (String), a `completed` status (Boolean, defaulting to false), and an automatically generated `createdAt` timestamp (Date). Mongoose will manage a collection named `tasks` in your MongoDB database for documents created using this `Task` model.

Basic CRUD Operations

With our `Task` model defined, we can now perform the fundamental database operations: Create, Read, Update, Delete (CRUD). Mongoose model methods are generally **asynchronous**, returning Promises. Using `async/await` makes working with them very clean.

Let's see how to use these in the context of controller functions (like those we set up in Chapter 5). Assume we have a `taskController.js`.

Create (Saving new documents)

To create a new task, you instantiate the model and call the `.save()` method on the instance.

```
// controllers/taskController.js (example function)
const Task = require('../models/Task'); // Import the model

const createTask = async (req, res, next) => {
  try {
    // req.body should contain { description: 'Buy milk', completed: false
(optional) }
    // Assumes body-parsing middleware (express.json()) is used in app.js
    const newTask = new Task(req.body);
    const savedTask = await newTask.save(); // Asynchronously save to DB
    res.status(201).json(savedTask); // Send back the created task
  } catch (error) {
    // Pass errors to the error handling middleware (Chapter 4)
    next(error);
  }
};
```

Read (Finding documents)

Mongoose provides several methods for finding documents:

- `Model.find(query)`: Finds all documents matching the `query` object (or all documents if the query is empty `{}`). Returns an array.
- `Model.findById(id)`: Finds a single document by its unique `_id`. Returns a single document or `null`.
- `Model.findOne(query)`: Finds the first document matching the `query`. Returns a single document or `null`.

```
// controllers/taskController.js (example functions)
const Task = require('../models/Task');

const getAllTasks = async (req, res, next) => {
  try {
    const tasks = await Task.find({}); // Find all tasks
    // We can now pass this data to a template (Chapter 6)
    // res.render('tasks/index', { tasks: tasks, pageTitle: 'All Tasks' });

    // Or send as JSON for an API
    res.status(200).json(tasks);
  } catch (error) {
```

```
      next(error);
  }
};

const getTaskById = async (req, res, next) => {
  try {
    const taskId = req.params.taskId; // Assuming route is like /tasks/:taskId
    const task = await Task.findById(taskId);
    if (!task) {
      // If task not found, send 404
      return res.status(404).json({ message: 'Task not found' });
    }
    res.status(200).json(task);
  } catch (error) {
    next(error);
  }
};
```

Update (Updating documents)

Methods like `Model.findByIdAndUpdate(id, updateData, options)` or `Model.updateOne(filter, updateData, options)` are common.

```
// controllers/taskController.js (example function)
const Task = require('../models/Task');

const updateTask = async (req, res, next) => {
  try {
    const taskId = req.params.taskId;
    // req.body might contain { description: '...', completed: true }
    const updateData = req.body;
    const options = { new: true, runValidators: true }; // Return updated doc,
run schema validators

    const updatedTask = await Task.findByIdAndUpdate(taskId, updateData,
options);

    if (!updatedTask) {
      return res.status(404).json({ message: 'Task not found' });
    }
    res.status(200).json(updatedTask);
  } catch (error) {
    next(error);
  }
};
```

Delete (Removing documents)

Use `Model.findByIdAndDelete(id)` or `Model.deleteOne(filter)`.

```
// controllers/taskController.js (example function)
const Task = require('../models/Task');

const deleteTask = async (req, res, next) => {
  try {
    const taskId = req.params.taskId;
    const deletedTask = await Task.findByIdAndDelete(taskId);

    if (!deletedTask) {
      return res.status(404).json({ message: 'Task not found' });
    }
    // Send 204 No Content for successful deletion often, or confirmation
message
    res.status(200).json({ message: 'Task deleted successfully' });
  } catch (error) {
    next(error);
  }
};
```

Integrating Database Operations with Routes

Now you connect these controller functions to your routes, typically defined in your routes directory (Chapter 5).

```
// routes/tasks.js
const express = require('express');
const router = express.Router();
const taskController = require('../controllers/taskController'); // Assuming you
have this file

// Define routes and map them to controller functions

// GET /tasks - Get all tasks
router.get('/', taskController.getAllTasks);

// POST /tasks - Create a new task
router.post('/', taskController.createTask);

// GET /tasks/:taskId - Get a single task by ID
router.get('/:taskId', taskController.getTaskById);
```

```
// PATCH /tasks/:taskId - Update a task by ID (PATCH often used for partial
updates)
router.patch('/:taskId', taskController.updateTask);

// DELETE /tasks/:taskId - Delete a task by ID
router.delete('/:taskId', taskController.deleteTask);

module.exports = router;
```

And finally, mount this router in your `app.js`:

```
// app.js
// ... (other setup)
const taskRouter = require('./routes/tasks');
app.use('/tasks', taskRouter); // Mount the task router
// ... (error handling, app.listen)
```

Now, requests to /tasks (and its sub-paths) will trigger the corresponding controller functions, which in turn interact with the MongoDB database via the Mongoose `Task` model using asynchronous operations. If you were rendering HTML (Chapter 6), your `getAllTasks` controller, instead of `res.json(tasks)`, would use `res.render('tasks', { tasks: tasks });`, passing the fetched data to your EJS template.

Chapter Summary

In this chapter, you learned why databases are essential for persistent data storage in web applications. We briefly compared relational (SQL) and NoSQL databases, choosing to focus on MongoDB, a popular document database, paired with the Mongoose ODM for easier interaction from Node.js.

You walked through the key steps: installing Mongoose and `dotenv`, connecting to your MongoDB instance securely using environment variables, defining data structure with Mongoose Schemas, and creating Models as your interface to database collections. We covered the fundamental asynchronous CRUD (Create, Read, Update, Delete) operations using Mongoose model methods like `.save()`, `.find()`, `.findById()`, `.findByIdAndUpdate()`, and `.findByIdAndDelete()`, emphasizing the use of `async/await` for cleaner code. Finally, you saw how to integrate these database operations into your Express application by calling model methods within your controller functions, which are then mapped to specific routes.

Your application can now not only generate dynamic pages but also store and retrieve the data needed for those pages from a persistent database. The next logical step is to allow users to *provide* that data. In the following chapter, we'll focus on handling HTML forms, enabling users to submit information (like new tasks, registration details, or search queries) to your server, which you can then validate and save to the database using the techniques learned here.

Chapter 8: Handling Forms and User Input

In the last chapter, we connected our Express application to a database using Mongoose, enabling us to store and retrieve persistent data like tasks. This gives our application memory and state. But how does data get *into* the database in the first place? While we can manually insert data or use API tools, most web applications interact with users through **HTML forms**. Forms are the standard way users submit information – registering for an account, posting a comment, searching for products, or, in our ongoing example, adding a new task. This chapter is all about receiving, processing, and validating that user input securely and effectively within your Express application. We'll leverage concepts like middleware (Chapter 4), routing (Chapter 5), templating (Chapter 6), and database interaction (Chapter 7) to build fully functional forms.

HTML Forms Review

Before diving into the server-side handling, let's quickly refresh our memory on the basic structure of an HTML form.

```html
<form action="/submit-task" method="POST">

  <label for="taskDesc">Task Description:</label>
  <input type="text" id="taskDesc" name="description" required>

  <label for="taskPriority">Priority:</label>
  <select id="taskPriority" name="priority">
    <option value="low">Low</option>
    <option value="medium" selected>Medium</option>
    <option value="high">High</option>
  </select>
```

```
<label>
  <input type="checkbox" name="isUrgent" value="true"> Is Urgent?
</label>

<textarea name="notes" placeholder="Add notes..."></textarea>

<button type="submit">Add Task</button>

</form>
```

Key elements and attributes:

- `<form>` **tag**: The container for the form inputs.
  - `action`: The URL path on the server where the form data should be sent when submitted (e.g., `/submit-task`).
  - `method`: The HTTP method to use for sending the data. The two most common values are:
    - `GET`: Appends the form data to the `action` URL as a query string. Suitable for non-sensitive data or actions that retrieve information (like search).
    - `POST`: Sends the form data in the body of the HTTP request. Preferred for submitting data that changes server state (like creating or updating records) or contains sensitive information.
- **Input Elements** (`<input>`, `<textarea>`, `<select>`): Where the user enters data.
  - `type`: Specifies the kind of input (e.g., `text`, `password`, `email`, `checkbox`, `radio`, `file`, `submit`).
  - `name`: **This is absolutely crucial!** The `name` attribute provides the key that the server-side code (Express) will use to identify the value submitted from this input field. Without a `name`, the data from that field won't be sent.
  - `id`: Used primarily for client-side scripting and associating `<label>` tags.
  - `value`: The data associated with the input (pre-filled for text, the value sent for checkboxes/radio buttons).
- `<label>` **tag**: Improves accessibility and usability by associating text with an input field (clicking the label often focuses the input).
- **Submit Button** (`<button type="submit">` **or** `<input type="submit">`): Triggers the form submission when clicked.

Processing GET Requests with Forms

When a form uses the `method="GET"`, the browser takes all the input fields with `name` attributes, creates key-value pairs (using the `name` as the key and the input's content as the value), and appends them to the `action` URL as a query string after a ?.

For example, if a search form looks like this:

```
<form action="/search" method="GET">
  <input type="text" name="query" placeholder="Search products...">
  <select name="category">
    <option value="">All</option>
    <option value="electronics">Electronics</option>
    <option value="books">Books</option>
  </select>
  <button type="submit">Search</button>
</form>
```

And the user types "laptop" and selects "Electronics", submitting the form will navigate the browser to a URL like: `http://yourdomain.com/search?query=laptop&category=electronics`.

In Express, you handle this just like any other GET request with query parameters, accessing the data via `req.query` (as we saw in Chapter 3):

```
// In your route handler for GET /search
app.get('/search', (req, res) => {
  const searchQuery = req.query.query || ''; // Default to empty string if
missing
  const category = req.query.category || 'All';

  console.log(`Searching for '${searchQuery}' in category '${category}'`);

  // Here you would typically query your database based on the search terms
  // and render a results page.
  res.send(`Displaying search results for "${searchQuery}" in category "$
{category}"`);
});
```

GET forms are ideal for things like search queries, filtering options, or any action where bookmarking the resulting URL or sharing it makes sense, as all the necessary parameters are right there in the URL. Avoid using GET for sensitive data (like passwords) or actions that modify data on the server.

Processing POST Requests with Forms

For actions that create or update data, or involve sensitive information, `method="POST"` is the standard choice. The form data is sent in the *body* of the HTTP request, not visibly in the URL.

However, Node.js (and Express by default) doesn't automatically parse the request body. Remember our discussion of middleware in Chapter 4? We need to use specific middleware to handle the incoming data format. For standard HTML forms submitted with POST, the data is usually sent with a `Content-Type` of `application/x-www-form-urlencoded`.

We use the built-in `express.urlencoded()` middleware for this:

```
// app.js (Make sure this is included BEFORE your routes that handle POST forms)
// Parses URL-encoded bodies (as sent by HTML forms)
app.use(express.urlencoded({ extended: true }));
// extended: true allows for richer objects/arrays, false uses simpler parsing.
// true is generally recommended unless you have specific reasons otherwise.

// If your forms might also submit JSON (less common for standard HTML forms,
// but possible with client-side JavaScript), include express.json() too:
// app.use(express.json());
```

Once this middleware is in place, Express will parse the incoming form data and make it available as a JavaScript object on `req.body`. The keys of the object will correspond to the `name` attributes of your form inputs.

Example: Adding a New Task

Let's build a form to add tasks to the database model we created in Chapter 7.

1. Display the Form (GET Request): First, we need a route to simply display the HTML form. We'll use EJS (Chapter 6) for this.

Create `views/tasks/new.ejs`:

```
<!-- views/tasks/new.ejs -->
<!DOCTYPE html>
<html lang="en">
<head>
  <meta charset="UTF-8">
  <title>Add New Task</title>
  <link rel="stylesheet" href="/css/style.css"> <!-- Link to your CSS -->
```

```
</head>
<body>
  <%- include('../partials/header') %> <!-- Include header if you have one -->

  <h1>Add a New Task</h1>

  <form action="/tasks" method="POST">
    <div>
      <label for="taskDesc">Description:</label>
      <input type="text" id="taskDesc" name="description" required>
    </div>
    <div>
      <label for="taskCompleted">Completed?</label>
      <input type="checkbox" id="taskCompleted" name="completed" value="true">
      <!-- Note: Unchecked checkboxes are NOT sent by the browser! -->
      <!-- We'll handle this server-side -->
    </div>
    <button type="submit">Add Task</button>
  </form>

  <%- include('../partials/footer') %> <!-- Include footer if you have one -->
</body>
</html>
```

Create a route (e.g., in routes/tasks.js) to render this view:

```
// routes/tasks.js (or wherever you handle task routes)
const express = require('express');
const router = express.Router();
const taskController = require('../controllers/taskController'); // Your
controller

// GET /tasks/new - Display form to add a new task
router.get('/new', (req, res) => {
  res.render('tasks/new', { pageTitle: 'Add Task' }); // Pass title if needed
});

// ... other task routes (POST /, GET /, GET /:id etc.) ...

module.exports = router;
```

2. Handle the Form Submission (POST Request): Now, we need the route handler for POST /tasks (defined by the form's action and method). This handler will use the taskController.createTask function we outlined in Chapter 7, which expects the data in req.body.

```
// controllers/taskController.js
const Task = require('../models/Task');

const createTask = async (req, res, next) => {
  try {
    // Thanks to express.urlencoded(), req.body contains the form data:
    // e.g., { description: 'User input text', completed: 'true' } (if checked)
    // or { description: 'User input text' } (if not checked)

    const taskData = {
      description: req.body.description,
      // Handle the checkbox: req.body.completed will be 'true' if checked,
      // or undefined if not checked. Convert to boolean.
      completed: req.body.completed === 'true'
    };

    const newTask = new Task(taskData);
    await newTask.save(); // Save to MongoDB

    // DON'T just send a response here. Redirect instead! (See PRG pattern)
    res.redirect('/tasks'); // Redirect to the task list page

  } catch (error) {
    console.error("Error creating task:", error);
    // Handle validation errors or other issues - more on this later
    // For now, pass to generic error handler
    next(error);
  }
};

// ... other controller functions (getAllTasks, etc.) ...

module.exports = { createTask, /* ... other functions */ };
```

Make sure the route is defined in routes/tasks.js:

```
// routes/tasks.js
// ... (GET /new) ...

// POST /tasks - Handle the form submission to create a task
router.post('/', taskController.createTask);

// GET / - Route to display all tasks (needed for the redirect)
router.get('/', taskController.getAllTasks); // Assume getAllTasks fetches and
renders a list
```

```
// ... (other routes) ...
```

The POST-Redirect-GET (PRG) Pattern:

Notice the `res.redirect('/tasks');` line in `createTask`. This is crucial. Why not just `res.send('Task created!')` or render the task list directly from the POST handler?

Imagine the user successfully submits the form. The server creates the task and sends back the "Task List" page. Now, what happens if the user hits the browser's **refresh** button? The browser might warn about resubmitting form data, but if the user clicks "OK", it will send the *exact same POST request* again, potentially creating a duplicate task!

The **POST-Redirect-GET (PRG)** pattern solves this:

1. **POST:** The user submits the form via POST.
2. **Redirect:** The server processes the POST request (e.g., saves the task). If successful, instead of sending HTML back directly, it sends an HTTP **redirect** response (status code 302 or 303) telling the browser to navigate to a *different* URL (usually the page displaying the newly created item or a list page, e.g., / tasks).
3. **GET:** The browser receives the redirect instruction and makes a *new* GET request to the specified URL (e.g., /tasks). This GET request handler then fetches the data (including the newly created task) and renders the appropriate page.

Now, if the user refreshes the page after the redirect, they are only refreshing the final GET request, which is safe and won't cause duplicate submissions. **Always use PRG after successful POST requests that modify data.**

Data Validation and Sanitization

You might have noticed the `required` attribute on the description input in our HTML form. That provides *client-side* validation – the browser might prevent submission if the field is empty. However, **you absolutely cannot rely solely on client-side validation.**

Why?

- Users can disable JavaScript.
- Malicious users can bypass browser validation entirely by crafting their own HTTP requests directly to your server (using tools like `curl` or Postman).

Server-side validation is non-negotiable. You must always validate incoming data in your Express application before trusting or saving it.

Basic Manual Validation

You can start with simple `if` checks in your controller:

```
// controllers/taskController.js (inside createTask)
const createTask = async (req, res, next) => {
  try {
    const description = req.body.description;

    // Basic server-side validation
    if (!description || description.trim().length === 0) {
      // Re-render the form with an error message
      return res.status(400).render('tasks/new', {
        pageTitle: 'Add Task',
        errorMessage: 'Task description cannot be empty.',
        // Pass back the invalid input so the user doesn't lose it
        taskData: { description: description } // Pass the entered data back
      });
    }
    if (description.length > 100) {
        return res.status(400).render('tasks/new', {
          pageTitle: 'Add Task',
          errorMessage: 'Task description must be 100 characters or less.',
          taskData: { description: description }
        });
    }

    const taskData = {
      description: description.trim(), // Trim whitespace before saving
      completed: req.body.completed === 'true'
    };

    const newTask = new Task(taskData);
    await newTask.save();
    res.redirect('/tasks');

  } catch (error) {
      // Mongoose validation errors can also be caught here
      if (error.name === 'ValidationError') {
        // Handle Mongoose validation errors (e.g., from the Schema)
        let errors = {};
        for (let field in error.errors) {
          errors[field] = error.errors[field].message;
        }
```

```
            return res.status(400).render('tasks/new', {
                pageTitle: 'Add Task',
                validationErrors: errors, // Pass specific field errors
                taskData: req.body // Pass original input back
            });
        }
        // Pass other errors to generic handler
        next(error);
    }
};
```

And update `views/tasks/new.ejs` to display errors and retain input:

```
<!-- views/tasks/new.ejs -->
<!-- ... (head, header) ... -->
<h1>Add a New Task</h1>

<%# Display generic error message %>
<% if (typeof errorMessage !== 'undefined' && errorMessage) { %>
  <p style="color: red;"><%= errorMessage %></p>
<% } %>

<%# Display Mongoose validation errors (if passed as validationErrors) %>
<% if (typeof validationErrors !== 'undefined') { %>
  <ul style="color: red;">
    <% Object.values(validationErrors).forEach(errMsg => { %>
      <li><%= errMsg %></li>
    <% }); %>
  </ul>
<% } %>

<form action="/tasks" method="POST">
  <div>
    <label for="taskDesc">Description:</label>
    <input type="text" id="taskDesc" name="description" required
           value="<%= (typeof taskData !== 'undefined') ? taskData.description :
'' %>">
    <%# Display specific error for this field %>
    <% if (typeof validationErrors !== 'undefined' &&
validationErrors.description) { %>
      <span style="color: red; font-size: 0.8em;"><%=
validationErrors.description %></span>
    <% } %>
  </div>
  <div>
    <label for="taskCompleted">Completed?</label>
```

```
  <input type="checkbox" id="taskCompleted" name="completed" value="true"
        <%= (typeof taskData !== 'undefined' && taskData.completed ===
'true') ? 'checked' : '' %>>
  </div>
  <button type="submit">Add Task</button>
</form>
<!-- ... (footer) ... -->
```

This works, but manual validation can become very verbose. Mongoose schema validation (like `required: true` in `models/Task.js`) helps, and you can catch those errors
in the `catch` block.

Using Validation Libraries (`express-validator`)

For more complex validation scenarios, libraries like `express-validator` provide a
much cleaner way to define and check validation rules using middleware.

1. **Install:** `npm install express-validator --save`
2. **Use:** You define validation chains (using functions like `body()`, `check()`,
   `isLength()`, `isEmail()`, `trim()`, etc.) and apply them as middleware *before*
   your route handler. Then, inside the handler, you check for errors using val-
   idationResult.

```
// routes/tasks.js
const express = require('express');
const router = express.Router();
const { body, validationResult } = require('express-validator'); // Import
const taskController = require('../controllers/taskController');

// Define validation rules as middleware
const taskValidationRules = [
  body('description')
    .notEmpty().withMessage('Task description cannot be empty.')
    .isLength({ max: 100 }).withMessage('Description max 100 chars.')
    .trim() // Also sanitizes by trimming whitespace
    .escape(), // Basic sanitization against XSS
  body('completed')
    .optional() // Allows it to be missing (for unchecked checkbox)
    .isBoolean().withMessage('Completed must be true or false.')
];

// POST /tasks - Apply validation middleware before the controller
router.post('/', taskValidationRules, taskController.createTaskWithValidation);
```

```
// ... other routes ...
module.exports = router;


// controllers/taskController.js
const Task = require('../models/Task');
const { validationResult } = require('express-validator'); // Import

const createTaskWithValidation = async (req, res, next) => {
  // Find validation errors in this request
  const errors = validationResult(req);
  if (!errors.isEmpty()) {
    // If there are errors, re-render the form with errors and old input
    return res.status(400).render('tasks/new', {
      pageTitle: 'Add Task',
      validationErrors: errors.mapped(), // Pass mapped errors object
      taskData: req.body // Pass original (potentially invalid) input back
    });
  }

  // If validation passed, proceed to create the task
  try {
    const taskData = {
      description: req.body.description,
      completed: req.body.completed === 'true' // Still need boolean conversion
    };
    const newTask = new Task(taskData);
    await newTask.save();
    res.redirect('/tasks');
  } catch (error) {
    // Handle potential database errors (duplicate keys, etc.)
    next(error);
  }
};

// Update views/tasks/new.ejs to display errors from errors.mapped() format
// (Check express-validator docs for error object structure)
```

express-validator offers a much more declarative and maintainable approach to validation and basic sanitization (like `trim()` and `escape()`).

Sanitization

Sanitization means cleaning or modifying user input to make it safe before storing or displaying it. The primary goal is often to prevent **Cross-Site Scripting (XSS)** attacks, where a malicious user injects harmful scripts into data that later gets rendered on a page for other users.

81

- **Output Escaping (Primary Defense):** As mentioned in Chapter 6, using `<%= %>` in EJS (or equivalent escaping in other template engines) is your *main defense* against XSS when *displaying* data. It converts characters like < and > into HTML entities (<, >), preventing them from being interpreted as HTML tags by the browser.
- **Input Sanitization:** Sometimes, you might also want to sanitize data *before* saving it to the database (e.g., stripping out all HTML tags, allowing only specific safe tags, or trimming whitespace). Libraries like `express-validator` provide basic sanitizers (`trim`, `escape`, `unescape`). For more advanced HTML sanitization, libraries like `dompurify` (often used with `jsdom` on the server) can be employed, although this adds complexity.

Prioritize output escaping, and apply input sanitization strategically where needed (e.g., trimming whitespace is almost always safe and useful).

Handling File Uploads

What if your form needs to allow users to upload files (like profile pictures, documents, etc.)? Standard form encoding (`application/x-www-form-urlencoded`) and body parsers (`express.urlencoded`, `express.json`) cannot handle file data.

When a form includes `<input type="file">`, you **must** set the form's encoding type to `multipart/form-data`:

```
<form action="/upload-profile-pic" method="POST" enctype="multipart/form-data">
  <label for="profilePic">Profile Picture:</label>
  <input type="file" id="profilePic" name="avatar" accept="image/*">
  <button type="submit">Upload</button>
</form>
```

To handle this `multipart/form-data` on the server, you need specific middleware. The most popular choice for Express is `multer`.

1. **Install:** `npm install multer --save`
2. **Configure and Use:** Multer acts as middleware, processing the incoming form data and making files available on `req.file` (for single file uploads) or `req.-files` (for multiple files). You typically configure where Multer should store the uploaded files.

```
// routes/uploads.js (Example)
const express = require('express');
```

```javascript
const multer = require('multer');
const path = require('path');
const router = express.Router();

// --- Multer Configuration ---
// Configure storage (can be memory or disk)
const storage = multer.diskStorage({
  destination: function (req, file, cb) {
    // Set the destination folder for uploads
    cb(null, 'uploads/'); // Make sure 'uploads/' directory exists!
  },
  filename: function (req, file, cb) {
    // Set the filename (use Date.now() to avoid name conflicts)
    const uniqueSuffix = Date.now() + '-' + Math.round(Math.random() * 1E9);
    cb(null, file.fieldname + '-' + uniqueSuffix +
path.extname(file.originalname));
  }
});

// Optional: File filter to accept only certain types
const fileFilter = (req, file, cb) => {
  if (file.mimetype === 'image/jpeg' || file.mimetype === 'image/png') {
    cb(null, true); // Accept file
  } else {
    cb(new Error('Invalid file type, only JPEG and PNG is allowed!'), false); //
Reject file
  }
};

// Initialize multer with storage options (and optional filter, limits)
const upload = multer({
  storage: storage,
  limits: {
    fileSize: 1024 * 1024 * 5 // Limit file size (e.g., 5MB)
  },
  fileFilter: fileFilter
});

// --- Route to Handle Single File Upload ---
// Use upload.single('fieldName') as middleware
// 'avatar' must match the 'name' attribute of the <input type="file">
router.post('/profile-pic', upload.single('avatar'), (req, res, next) => {
  // If multer encounters an error (e.g., file too large, wrong type),
  // it might pass an error to the next handler. Need error handling.

  if (!req.file) {
    // Handle case where no file was uploaded but form was submitted
```

```
        return res.status(400).send('No file uploaded.');
    }

    console.log('File uploaded successfully!');
    console.log('File info:', req.file);
    // req.file contains information like path, filename, mimetype, size

    // Here you would typically save the file path (req.file.path)
    // to a user record in your database.

    res.send(`Profile picture uploaded! Path: ${req.file.path}`);

}, (error, req, res, next) => {
    // Multer error handling middleware (specific to this route)
    if (error instanceof multer.MulterError) {
        // A Multer error occurred when uploading.
        console.error("Multer Error:", error);
        res.status(400).send(`File Upload Error: ${error.message}`);
    } else if (error) {
        // An unknown error occurred when uploading.
        console.error("Unknown Upload Error:", error);
        res.status(500).send(`File Upload Error: ${error.message || 'Unknown
error'}`);
    } else {
        next(); // Should not happen if error handler is only for errors
    }
});


// Example for multiple files (e.g., <input type="file" name="gallery"
multiple>)
// router.post('/gallery', upload.array('gallery', 10), (req, res, next) => {
//    // Access files via req.files (an array)
//    console.log(req.files);
//    res.send(`${req.files.length} gallery images uploaded!`);
// }, /* Add error handler here too */ );


module.exports = router;
```

Security Considerations for File Uploads:

- **Validate File Types:** Use `fileFilter` (as shown) or check `req.file.mimetype` server-side. Don't rely only on the browser's `accept` attribute.
- **Limit File Size:** Use `limits.fileSize` to prevent denial-of-service attacks using huge files.

- **Set Secure Filenames:** Don't trust the user-provided filename directly. Generate unique filenames (like using `Date.now()` or UUIDs) to avoid conflicts and potential path traversal issues.
- **Store Files Safely:** Store uploaded files *outside* your web root if possible, or in a directory with restricted permissions. Access them via a dedicated route that checks permissions before serving the file. Don't store them directly in your `/public` directory if they contain sensitive information. Consider cloud storage services (like AWS S3, Google Cloud Storage) for production applications.
- **Scan for Malware:** For applications requiring higher security, consider integrating malware scanning for uploaded files.

Chapter Summary

This chapter equipped you to handle the essential flow of user input through HTML forms in your Express applications. You reviewed the basics of HTML forms, including the `action`, `method`, and crucial `name` attributes. We contrasted handling `GET` requests (data in `req.query`) with `POST` requests (data in `req.body`).

You learned the importance of using body-parsing middleware like `express.urlencoded()` for POST requests and how to access the submitted data via `req.body`. We walked through a practical example of creating a form, displaying it with EJS, and handling its submission to save data to a database (using our Task model from Chapter 7). Crucially, we implemented the **POST-Redirect-GET (PRG)** pattern using `res.redirect()` to prevent duplicate form submissions.

We stressed the critical need for **server-side validation**, demonstrating manual checks and introducing the more robust `express-validator` library. You also learned about **sanitization** as a defense against XSS attacks, complementing the primary defense of output escaping in templates (`<%= %>`). Finally, we tackled **file uploads**, setting the correct form `enctype`, using the `multer` middleware to process `multipart/form-data`, accessing file information on `req.file/req.files`, and highlighting important security considerations.

Your application can now interact with users, accept their input, validate it, and store it persistently. However, how does the application remember who is who between different requests? How do you ensure only logged-in users can add tasks or upload profile pictures? In the next chapter, we'll explore **sessions and authentication**, enabling your application to manage user state and secure specific routes.

Chapter 9: Sessions and Authentication

We've come a long way! Your Express application can now handle user input via forms (Chapter 8), validate that input, and store it persistently in a database (Chapter 7). Users can add tasks, and maybe soon, register accounts or post comments. But there's a fundamental piece missing. When a user adds task A, and another user adds task B moments later, how does the server know which user added which task? How can we show a user *only* their own tasks? How do we prevent anyone from accessing a page meant only for registered users?

The core issue is that **HTTP, the protocol of the web, is inherently stateless**. Each request a browser makes to your server is treated as an independent event, completely separate from any previous requests. The server, by default, has no memory of who made the last request or the one before that. To build personalized and secure applications, we need mechanisms to:

1. **Maintain State (Sessions):** Remember information about a specific user across multiple requests.
2. **Verify Identity (Authentication):** Confirm that users are who they claim to be (e.g., by checking a username and password).
3. **Control Access (Authorization):** Determine what actions an authenticated user is allowed to perform (e.g., only admins can access certain pages - though we'll focus primarily on authentication here).

This chapter dives into managing user state with sessions and implementing basic user authentication in Express.

The Stateless Nature of HTTP

Imagine walking into a shop. Every time you ask the shopkeeper a question ("Where are the apples?", "How much is this?"), they answer you but instantly forget who you are the moment you finish speaking. The next time you ask something, it's as if they've never seen you before. That's HTTP!

This statelessness was fine for the early web of simple document fetching, but it's impractical for applications where context matters. We need the server "shopkeeper" to remember us between requests, at least for a while. How can we achieve this? The most common solutions involve cookies and sessions.

Cookies vs. Sessions

Both cookies and sessions aim to solve the state problem, but they work differently:

Cookies

- **How they work:** When the server wants to store a small piece of information (like a user ID or preference), it sends a `Set-Cookie` header in its response. The browser receives this instruction and stores the data (the cookie) locally. On subsequent requests *to the same domain*, the browser automatically includes the stored cookie data in a `Cookie` header sent back to the server.
- **Storage:** Client-side (in the user's browser).
- **Pros:** Simple to implement for small amounts of non-sensitive data.
- **Cons:**
    - **Size Limit:** Cookies have size restrictions (usually around 4KB).
    - **Security Risk:** Cookies are stored on the user's machine, often in plain text. Users can view and potentially modify them. Storing sensitive data directly in cookies is generally insecure.
    - **Sent with Every Request:** Cookies matching the domain are sent with *every* request (including requests for images, CSS, etc.), adding overhead.

Sessions

- **How they work:** Sessions take a more secure, server-centric approach.
    1. When a user first interacts in a way that requires a session (e.g., logging in), the server generates a **unique Session ID** (a long, random, hard-to-guess string).
    2. The server stores the actual session data (e.g., user ID, shopping cart contents) on the **server-side**, associated with that unique Session ID. This storage can be server memory (for development), a database, or a dedicated cache like Redis.

3. The server sends *only* the unique Session ID back to the browser, typically stored in a **cookie**.
4. On subsequent requests, the browser sends the Session ID cookie back to the server.
5. The server extracts the Session ID from the cookie, looks up the corresponding session data in its server-side store, and makes that data available to your application logic (usually via an object like `req.session`).

- **Storage:** Primarily server-side; only a small Session ID cookie is stored client-side.
- **Pros:**
  1. **More Secure:** Sensitive data stays on the server, not exposed in the browser.
  2. **Larger Data:** Server-side storage isn't subject to cookie size limits.
  3. **More Control:** The server manages the session lifecycle.
- **Cons:** Requires server-side storage resources.

For most authentication and user state management in traditional web applications, **sessions are the preferred method** due to their enhanced security.

Implementing Sessions with `express-session`

Express provides excellent support for sessions through the `express-session` middleware.

1. **Install:** Add it to your project:

```
npm install express-session --save
# Or: npm install express-session
```

2. **Configure and Use:** You need to configure and apply the middleware using `app.use()`. This should typically happen **before** any routes that need to access session data.

```
// app.js
const session = require('express-session');
require('dotenv').config(); // Ensure dotenv is loaded for secret

// --- Session Configuration ---
app.use(session({
  // Secret used to sign the session ID cookie.
```

```javascript
    // Should be a long, random string stored securely in environment
variables.
    secret: process.env.SESSION_SECRET || 'a default secret (change me!)',

    // Forces the session to be saved back to the session store, even if
    // the session was never modified during the request. Default is true,
    // but false is generally recommended unless needed for specific store
behaviors.
    resave: false,

    // Forces a session that is "uninitialized" to be saved to the store.
    // A session is uninitialized when it is new but not modified.
    // Setting this to false is useful for implementing login sessions,
reducing
    // server storage usage, and complying with laws that require
permission
    // before setting a cookie.
    saveUninitialized: false,

    // --- Cookie Configuration ---
    cookie: {
        // maxAge: Sets the expiration time in milliseconds (e.g., 1 hour)
        // maxAge: 1000 * 60 * 60 * 1, // 1 hour
        // By default, it's a session cookie (deleted when browser closes)

        // httpOnly: If true, prevents client-side JS from accessing the
cookie.
        // Crucial security measure against XSS attacks stealing session
IDs.
        httpOnly: true,

        // secure: If true, the browser will only send the cookie over
HTTPS.
        // Set to true in production if your site uses HTTPS.
        // For development over HTTP, keep it false or it won't work.
        secure: process.env.NODE_ENV === 'production' // Example: use secure
in prod only
    }
    // --- Session Store Configuration (See below) ---
    // store: mySessionStore // Add this later for production
}));

// --- Important Placement ---
// Place session middleware BEFORE routers/routes that need it.
// app.use('/users', userRouter);
// app.use('/tasks', taskRouter);
```

Key Configuration Options:

- `secret`: **Absolutely critical!** This string is used to sign the session ID cookie, preventing tampering. Treat it like a password – keep it complex, random, and store it securely in an environment variable (like `SESSION_SECRET` loaded via `dotenv`), not hardcoded.
- `resave: false`: Usually the best option. Avoids unnecessary session saves on every request.
- `saveUninitialized: false`: Good practice for login sessions. Only create a session cookie once the user actually logs in or session data is added.
- `cookie.httpOnly: true`: **Essential security setting.** Prevents JavaScript running in the browser from reading the session cookie, mitigating XSS risks.
- `cookie.secure: true` (in production): Ensures the session cookie is only sent over encrypted HTTPS connections.

Session Stores

By default, `express-session` uses an in-memory store (`MemoryStore`). This is fine for development, but it has major drawbacks for production:

- It leaks memory over time and is not designed for production loads.
- All session data is lost if the server restarts or crashes.
- It doesn't scale if you run multiple instances of your application server (each instance would have its own separate memory store).

For production, you **must** use a persistent session store, typically backed by a database or cache. Common choices include:

- **Database Stores:** Store session data in your application database.
  - `connect-mongo`: For MongoDB.
  - `connect-pg-simple`: For PostgreSQL.
  - Other connectors exist for MySQL, SQLite, etc.
- **Cache Stores:** Store session data in fast in-memory caches like Redis.
  - `connect-redis`: For Redis.

Let's integrate `connect-mongo` assuming you're using MongoDB (as set up in Chapter 7).

1. **Install:** `npm install connect-mongo --save`

2. **Configure**: Pass an instance of the store to the `express-session` configuration.

```
// app.js
const session = require('express-session');
const MongoStore = require('connect-mongo'); // Import connect-mongo
require('dotenv').config();

// Make sure Mongoose connection is established BEFORE setting up session store
// (Assuming connectDB from Chapter 7 is called earlier)
const connectDB = require('./config/db'); // Assuming you have db connection
setup
connectDB();

// --- Session Configuration with MongoStore ---
app.use(session({
  secret: process.env.SESSION_SECRET || 'a default secret (change me!)',
  resave: false,
  saveUninitialized: false,
  store: MongoStore.create({
    // Use the MONGODB_URI from your .env file
    mongoUrl: process.env.MONGODB_URI,
    // Optional: set collection name, TTL (time-to-live for sessions)
    // collectionName: 'sessions',
    // ttl: 14 * 24 * 60 * 60 // = 14 days. Default is null (no expiry)
  }),
  cookie: {
    // maxAge: 1000 * 60 * 60 * 24, // Example: 1 day persistence for cookie
    httpOnly: true,
    secure: process.env.NODE_ENV === 'production'
  }
}));

// ... (rest of app setup) ...
```

Now, session data will be stored persistently in a `sessions` collection in your MongoDB database.

Accessing and Modifying Session Data

Once the session middleware is active, every request object (`req`) will have a `req.session` property. You can read from and write properties to this object freely. The middleware automatically handles saving the changes to the session store and setting the cookie.

```
// Example route handler
app.get('/view-counter', (req, res) => {
  if (req.session.views) {
    req.session.views++; // Increment the views count
  } else {
    req.session.views = 1; // Initialize if it's the first visit
  }
  res.send(`You have visited this page ${req.session.views} times in this
session.`);
});
```

Destroying Sessions

To log a user out or explicitly end a session, use `req.session.destroy()`. This removes the session data from the store. It takes an optional callback function that runs after the session is destroyed.

```
// Example logout route handler
app.get('/logout', (req, res, next) => {
  req.session.destroy((err) => {
    if (err) {
      // Handle error case, maybe log it or pass to error handler
      return next(err);
    }
    // Redirect to home page or login page after logout
    res.redirect('/');
  });
});
```

Basic Authentication Strategy: Username/Password

Now let's use sessions to implement a classic username/password authentication flow.

1. User Model: You'll need a User model (similar to the Task model from Chapter 7) to store user credentials in your database. Crucially, it must include fields for a username (or email) and a **hashed password**.

```
// models/User.js
const mongoose = require('mongoose');
const bcrypt = require('bcrypt'); // Import bcrypt
```

```javascript
const userSchema = new mongoose.Schema({
  username: {
    type: String,
    required: [true, 'Username is required'],
    unique: true, // Ensure usernames are unique
    trim: true,
    lowercase: true
  },
  password: {
    type: String,
    required: [true, 'Password is required']
    // Add minlength validation if desired
  }
  // Add other fields like email, name, createdAt, etc.
});


// --- Password Hashing Middleware ---
// Use Mongoose 'pre save' middleware to automatically hash the password
// BEFORE a user document is saved to the database.
userSchema.pre('save', async function(next) {
  // Only hash the password if it has been modified (or is new)
  if (!this.isModified('password')) return next();

  try {
    // Generate a salt (randomness factor) - 10 rounds is generally recommended
    const salt = await bcrypt.genSalt(10);
    // Hash the password with the salt
    this.password = await bcrypt.hash(this.password, salt);
    next();
  } catch (error) {
    next(error); // Pass error to Mongoose/Express error handling
  }
});


// --- Password Comparison Method ---
// Add a method to the userSchema to compare submitted password with stored hash
userSchema.methods.comparePassword = async function(candidatePassword) {
  try {
    // Use bcrypt.compare to securely compare plain text pass with hash
    const isMatch = await bcrypt.compare(candidatePassword, this.password);
    return isMatch;
  } catch (error) {
    throw error; // Re-throw error to be caught by caller
  }
};

const User = mongoose.model('User', userSchema);
```

```
module.exports = User;
```

Important Security Note: Password Hashing

Never, EVER store passwords in plain text in your database! If your database is ever compromised, attackers will have direct access to all user passwords.

We use the `bcrypt` library (install with `npm install bcrypt`) to securely hash passwords.

- **Hashing**: A one-way process that converts a password into a fixed-length string (the hash). It's computationally infeasible to reverse the hash back into the original password.
- **Salting**: Before hashing, bcrypt generates a unique random string (a "salt") for each password. This salt is stored along with the hash. Salting ensures that even if two users have the same password, their stored hashes will be different, preventing attackers from using precomputed "rainbow tables" to crack passwords.

The `userSchema.pre('save', ...)` middleware automatically handles hashing *before* saving. The `comparePassword` method provides a safe way to check if a submitted password matches the stored hash during login.

2. Registration:

- **Form:** Create an EJS view (`views/auth/register.ejs`) with fields for username and password.
- **GET Route:** A route to display the registration form.
- **POST Route Handler:**
    - Receive `username` and `password` from `req.body` (use `express.urlencoded`).
    - Perform validation (e.g., using `express-validator` or manually). Check if username already exists.
    - Create a new User instance: `const newUser = new User({ username, password });`
    - Save the user: `await newUser.save();`. The `pre('save')` hook in the model will automatically hash the password.
    - Redirect to the login page or maybe automatically log them in (see step 3). Use PRG!

3. Login:

- **Form:** Create an EJS view (`views/auth/login.ejs`) with fields for username and password.
- **GET Route:** A route to display the login form.
- **POST Route Handler:**
  - Receive `username` and `password` from `req.body`.
  - **Find User:** Look up the user in the database by username: `const user = await User.findOne({ username: req.body.username });`
  - **Check User Exists:** If `!user`, the user wasn't found. Re-render the login form with an error message ("Invalid credentials").
  - **Compare Passwords:** If user exists, use the model method: `const isMatch = await user.comparePassword(req.body.password);`
  - **Check Match:** If `!isMatch`, the password was incorrect. Re-render the login form with an error ("Invalid credentials"). **Do not tell the user specifically whether the username or password was wrong** - this helps prevent username enumeration attacks.
  - **Success:** If `isMatch` is true, the credentials are valid!
    - **Store in Session:** Store identifying information in the session: `req.session.userId = user._id;` (Storing just the ID is common). You could also store the username `req.session.username = user.username;`.
    - Redirect the user to their dashboard or a protected page (e.g., `/tasks`). Use PRG!

```
// controllers/authController.js (Example Login Handler)
const User = require('../models/User');

const loginUser = async (req, res, next) => {
  const { username, password } = req.body;

  try {
    // 1. Find user by username (case-insensitive recommended)
    const user = await User.findOne({ username: username.toLowerCase() });

    // 2. Check if user exists and password is correct
    if (!user || !(await user.comparePassword(password))) {
      // Invalid credentials - re-render login form with generic error
      // Use flash messages here! (See below)
      console.log('Invalid login attempt'); // Log for debugging
      return res.status(401).render('auth/login', {
        pageTitle: 'Login',
        errorMessage: 'Invalid username or password.'
      });
```

```
    }

    // 3. Credentials are valid - Store user ID in session
    req.session.userId = user._id;
    req.session.username = user.username; // Optional: store username too

    // Ensure session is saved before redirecting (optional but can help avoid
race conditions)
    req.session.save((err) => {
        if (err) {
            return next(err);
        }
        // 4. Redirect to a protected area (e.g., dashboard or task list)
        res.redirect('/tasks'); // Redirect to their tasks page
    });

  } catch (error) {
    next(error);
  }
};

module.exports = { loginUser, /* other auth functions */ };
```

Protecting Routes (Authorization Middleware)

Now that users can log in and have their `userId` stored in the session, we need to restrict access to certain routes. We do this by creating **authorization middleware**.

```
// middleware/authMiddleware.js (Example)

const requireLogin = (req, res, next) => {
  // Check if the userId property exists on the session object
  if (!req.session.userId) {
    // If not logged in, redirect to the login page
    return res.redirect('/login'); // Adjust '/login' path if needed
  }
  // If logged in (userId exists in session), proceed to the next middleware or
route handler
  next();
};

module.exports = { requireLogin };
```

You can then apply this middleware:

- **To specific routes:**

```
// routes/tasks.js
const { requireLogin } = require('../middleware/authMiddleware');
// ...
// Apply middleware only to routes that need authentication
router.get('/', requireLogin, taskController.getAllTasks);
router.post('/', requireLogin, taskController.createTask);
router.get('/new', requireLogin, taskController.showNewTaskForm);
// Maybe GET /:taskId is public, but PATCH/DELETE require login?
router.get('/:taskId', taskController.getTaskById); // Public?
router.patch('/:taskId', requireLogin, taskController.updateTask);
router.delete('/:taskId', requireLogin, taskController.deleteTask);
```

- **To an entire router:** (Useful for sections like /admin or /account)

```
// app.js
const { requireLogin } = require('./middleware/authMiddleware');
const accountRouter = require('./routes/account');
// All routes defined within accountRouter now require login
app.use('/account', requireLogin, accountRouter);
```

Now, if a user tries to access /tasks or /account without having logged in (i.e., without a userId in their session), they will be automatically redirected to /login.

Using Flash Messages

When we handle login failures or successful registrations/logouts, we often redirect the user. But how do we show a one-time message on the *next* page they see (e.g., "Invalid username or password" on the login page after a failed attempt, or "Logout successful!" on the home page)? Session data persists, so just setting a session variable won't work well for these temporary notifications.

This is the perfect use case for **flash messages**. They are stored in the session but are designed to be retrieved and cleared *only once*. The connect-flash middleware makes this easy.

1. **Install:** npm install connect-flash --save

2. **Configure:** Initialize it *after* the express-session middleware.

```
// app.js
const session = require('express-session');
```

```
const flash = require('connect-flash'); // Import
// ... other requires ...

// ... (session configuration) ...
app.use(session({...}));

// --- Flash Message Middleware ---
// Must be after session middleware
app.use(flash());

// Optional: Custom middleware to make flash messages available
// directly in templates (res.locals) for easier access in views.
app.use((req, res, next) => {
  // Get flash messages from the session
  res.locals.success_messages = req.flash('success');
  res.locals.error_messages = req.flash('error');
  // You can define other types too (e.g., 'info', 'warning')
  next();
});

// ... (routers, error handling, listen) ...
```

3. **Setting Messages:** Before redirecting in your route handlers, call `req.flash('type', 'message')`. The `type` is a category you define (e.g., success, error).

```
// controllers/authController.js (Inside loginUser, on failure)
if (!user || !(await user.comparePassword(password))) {
    req.flash('error', 'Invalid username or password.'); // Set flash
message
    return res.redirect('/login'); // Redirect back to login page
}
// On successful login:
req.flash('success', 'You are now logged in!'); // Set flash message
res.redirect('/tasks');

// controllers/authController.js (Example logout handler)
req.session.destroy((err) => {
    if (err) return next(err);
    req.flash('success', 'You have been logged out.'); // Set flash
message
    res.redirect('/');
});
```

4. **Displaying Messages:** In your EJS views (often in a header partial so messages appear on all pages), check for the presence of messages in `res.locals` (made available by our custom middleware) and display them.

```
<!-- views/partials/header.ejs (or wherever you want messages) -->
<%# Display Success Flash Messages %>
<% if (success_messages && success_messages.length > 0) { %>
  <div class="alert alert-success" role="alert"> <%# Use appropriate CSS
classes %>
    <% success_messages.forEach(msg => { %>
      <p><%= msg %></p>
    <% }); %>
  </div>
<% } %>

<%# Display Error Flash Messages %>
<% if (error_messages && error_messages.length > 0) { %>
  <div class="alert alert-danger" role="alert"> <%# Use appropriate CSS
classes %>
    <% error_messages.forEach(msg => { %>
      <p><%= msg %></p>
    <% }); %>
  </div>
<% } %>
```

Now, temporary messages will appear correctly after redirects and disappear on the next request.

Chapter Summary

This chapter tackled the crucial concepts of state management and user identity in stateless HTTP. You learned the difference between cookies (client-side storage) and sessions (server-side storage with a client-side ID cookie), understanding why sessions are generally preferred for security.

We implemented sessions using the `express-session` middleware, covering essential configuration options like `secret`, `resave`, `saveUninitialized`, and cookie settings (`httpOnly`, `secure`). You learned the importance of using persistent session stores (like `connect-mongo`) for production environments.

We then built a basic username/password authentication system. This involved creating a User model, emphasizing the absolute necessity of **hashing passwords** securely using `bcrypt` before storage. You saw the registration and login flow, including finding users, comparing submitted passwords with stored hashes using `bcrypt.compare()`, and storing user identifiers (like `userId`) in `req.session` upon successful login.

To secure parts of the application, you created authorization middleware (`requireLogin`) that checks for the presence of `req.session.userId` and redirects unauthenticated users. Finally, we introduced `connect-flash` to handle temporary, one-time notification messages (flash messages) across redirects, improving the user experience for actions like login success/failure or logout.

Your application can now securely manage user sessions and control access based on authentication status. While session-based authentication is ideal for server-rendered web applications, modern web development often involves separate frontend applications (like Single Page Apps built with React, Vue, or Angular) communicating with backend APIs. These APIs typically use different authentication mechanisms, often token-based. In the next chapter, we'll shift our focus to building **RESTful APIs** with Express, preparing your backend to serve data not just to EJS templates, but to any kind of client application.

Chapter 10: Building RESTful APIs

Up to this point, we've focused primarily on using Express to build traditional web applications where the server generates HTML (often using templating engines like EJS, as covered in Chapter 6) and sends it directly to the browser. This is a perfectly valid and common way to build websites. However, the modern web often involves richer client-side interactions driven by JavaScript frameworks (like React, Vue, Angular) or native mobile applications. These clients don't usually want fully formed HTML pages from the server; instead, they need raw **data** they can process and display themselves.

This is where **APIs (Application Programming Interfaces)** come in. An API acts as a contract, defining how different software components should communicate. In web development, this typically means a backend API (built with Node.js/Express!) exposing data and functionality to various frontend clients over HTTP. Instead of sending HTML, the API usually sends data formatted in **JSON (JavaScript Object Notation)**.

Express is exceptionally well-suited for building APIs. Its minimalist nature and robust routing/middleware system (Chapters 3, 4, 5) make it easy to define endpoints that serve data. The most common architectural style for designing these web APIs is **REST (Representational State Transfer)**. In this chapter, we'll shift gears from server-side rendering to building RESTful APIs with Express, enabling your backend to communicate effectively with any kind of client.

What is an API? What is REST?

- **API (Application Programming Interface):** At a high level, an API is simply a set of rules and definitions that allow different software systems to communicate with each other. It defines the kinds of requests that can be made, how to make them, the data formats that should be used, and the kinds of responses to expect. Think of it like a menu at a restaurant: it tells you what dishes (data/functionality) you can order and how to order them (the specific request format).

- **REST (Representational State Transfer):** REST is not a strict protocol or standard like HTTP, but rather an **architectural style** for designing networked applications, particularly web services. It was defined by Roy Fielding in his doctoral dissertation in 2000. REST provides a set of constraints or principles that, when followed, lead to systems that are scalable, reliable, and easy to evolve. APIs designed according to these principles are often called **RESTful APIs**.

While REST has several guiding principles, some of the most important ones for understanding web APIs are:

1. **Client-Server Architecture:** The client (e.g., browser, mobile app) and the server are separate entities that communicate over a network. The server manages data and logic; the client manages the user interface and user experience. This separation allows them to evolve independently.
2. **Statelessness:** This is a key differentiator from the session-based applications we built in Chapter 9. In a RESTful API, **each request from the client to the server must contain all the information the server needs to understand and fulfill the request.** The server should not store any client context (session state) between requests. If authentication is needed, the client must send credentials or a token with *every* protected request. This constraint enhances scalability (any server instance can handle any request) and reliability.
3. **Uniform Interface:** This is arguably the core of REST and includes several sub-constraints:
    - **Resource Identification:** Resources (e.g., a user, a task, a product) are identified by URIs (Uniform Resource Identifiers) – essentially, the URL paths (e.g., `/users/123`, `/tasks`).
    - **Resource Manipulation Through Representations:** Clients interact with resources by exchanging *representations* of those resources. The most common representation format on the web today is JSON. When a client wants to update a task, it sends a JSON representation of the desired state to the server.
    - **Self-Descriptive Messages:** Each request/response should contain enough information for the other party to understand it (e.g., using standard HTTP methods, status codes, and headers like `Content-Type` to indicate the format of the body).

- **Hypermedia as the Engine of Application State (HATEOAS):** (Often considered the most complex and least strictly followed principle). The idea is that responses from the server should include links (hypermedia) that tell the client what other actions they can take next. This allows clients to navigate the API dynamically.

Building truly "RESTful" APIs (especially adhering strictly to HATEOAS) can be complex. Many APIs you encounter are more accurately described as "REST-like" or "HTTP APIs," primarily leveraging resource-based URLs and standard HTTP methods. For our purposes, understanding resource identification, statelessness, and using standard methods/JSON representations is key.

Designing API Endpoints

How do you structure the URLs (endpoints) for your API? RESTful design principles provide helpful guidelines:

- **Focus on Resources (Nouns):** Endpoints should represent the *things* (resources) your API manages, not the actions. Use nouns, preferably plural.
    - *Good:* `/tasks`, `/users`, `/products`
    - *Bad:* `/getAllTasks`, `/createNewUser`, `/deleteProductById`
- **Use HTTP Methods for Actions:** The standard HTTP methods map naturally to CRUD (Create, Read, Update, Delete) operations on your resources:
    - `GET`: Retrieve resources. Should be safe (no side effects) and idempotent (multiple identical requests have the same effect as one).
        - `GET /tasks`: Retrieve a list of all tasks.
        - `GET /tasks/123`: Retrieve task with ID 123.
    - `POST`: Create a new resource. Not usually idempotent (multiple identical requests may create multiple resources).
        - `POST /tasks`: Create a new task (data sent in the request body).
    - `PUT`: Replace an existing resource entirely with the data provided in the request body. Should be idempotent.
        - `PUT /tasks/123`: Replace the entire task with ID 123 with the new data.
    - `PATCH`: Partially update an existing resource with the data provided. Not necessarily idempotent.
        - `PATCH /tasks/123`: Update only specific fields (e.g., `completed` status) of task 123. (Often preferred over PUT for updates).
    - `DELETE`: Remove a resource. Should be idempotent.
        - `DELETE /tasks/123`: Delete task with ID 123.

- **Use URL Parameters for Specific Resources:** Use path parameters (like `:taskId` in Express, accessed via `req.params`) to identify specific resource instances. Use query parameters (`req.query`) for filtering, sorting, or pagination of collections.
  - `GET /tasks/123` (Specific task)
  - `GET /tasks?completed=true&sortBy=createdAt` (Filter and sort)
- **Versioning:** APIs evolve. To avoid breaking existing clients when you make changes, it's crucial to version your API. Common strategies include:
  - **URL Path Versioning (Most Common):** Include the version number in the URL prefix, e.g., `/api/v1/tasks`, `/api/v2/tasks`. This is clear and easy to manage.
  - **Query Parameter Versioning:** `/api/tasks?version=1` (Less common).
  - **Custom Header Versioning:** Use a custom request header like `Accept-Version: v1` (Clean, but less visible).

We'll use URL path versioning (`/api/v1/...`) in our examples.

Sending JSON Responses

When building an API, instead of `res.render()` or `res.sendFile()`, you'll primarily use `res.json()` (introduced in Chapter 3). This method automatically:

- Serializes JavaScript objects or arrays into a JSON string.
- Sets the `Content-Type` response header to `application/json`.

It's good practice to standardize the structure of your API responses for consistency. This makes it easier for clients to parse and handle them. A common approach is to use a wrapper object:

```
// Example Successful Response Structure
{
  "status": "success",
  "data": {
    // Actual data payload goes here (e.g., a single task object or an array of
tasks)
    "task": { "_id": "...", "description": "...", "completed": false }
  }
}
// Or for a list:
{
  "status": "success",
  "results": 15, // Optional: number of items returned
  "data": {
```

```
       "tasks": [ /* array of task objects */ ]
  }
}


// Example Error Response Structure
{
  "status": "fail", // Or "error"
  "message": "Resource not found.", // Human-readable error message
  "errorCode": "RESOURCE_NOT_FOUND" // Optional: machine-readable code
}
// Or for validation errors:
{
  "status": "fail",
  "message": "Validation failed.",
  "errors": {
    "description": "Task description cannot be empty.",
    "priority": "Invalid priority value."
  }
}
```

Always accompany your JSON responses with appropriate HTTP status codes using `res.status()`:

- `200 OK`: General success for GET, PATCH, PUT (if no content returned).
- `201 Created`: Successful creation of a resource (after POST). Often includes the created resource in the response body.
- `204 No Content`: Successful request, but no content to return (e.g., after a successful DELETE). The response body *must* be empty.
- `400 Bad Request`: Client error (e.g., invalid JSON format, missing required fields, failed validation).
- `401 Unauthorized`: Authentication is required and has failed or not been provided.
- `403 Forbidden`: Authenticated user does not have permission to access the resource.
- `404 Not Found`: The requested resource could not be found.
- `500 Internal Server Error`: A generic error occurred on the server. Don't reveal sensitive stack traces in production!

Receiving JSON Data

Just as your API sends JSON, it often needs to *receive* JSON data from clients, typically in the body of POST, PUT, or PATCH requests.

As covered in Chapter 4, you need the `express.json()` middleware enabled in your application setup to parse incoming JSON request bodies.

```
// app.js
// Make sure this middleware is applied before your API routes
app.use(express.json());
```

Clients sending JSON data **must** set the `Content-Type` request header to `application/json`. When they do, and the `express.json()` middleware is active, the parsed JSON object will be available on `req.body` in your route handlers.

Implementing CRUD Operations for an API

Let's adapt the database operations for our `Task` model (from Chapter 7) to create RESTful API endpoints. We'll organize these under an `/api/v1/tasks` path using `express.Router` (Chapter 5).

1. Create API Router: Create `routes/api/v1/tasks.js` (you might need `api` and `v1` subdirectories within `routes`).

2. Create/Adapt Controller: Create `controllers/api/v1/taskApiController.js` (or similar). Adapt the functions from `taskController.js` to send JSON responses instead of rendering views or redirecting.

```
// controllers/api/v1/taskApiController.js
const Task = require('../../../models/Task'); // Adjust path as needed

// GET /api/v1/tasks - Get all tasks
const getAllTasks = async (req, res, next) => {
  try {
    // Basic filtering example (e.g., /api/v1/tasks?completed=true)
    const queryObj = { ...req.query };
    const excludedFields = ['sort', 'page', 'limit', 'fields']; // For potential
future features
    excludedFields.forEach(el => delete queryObj[el]);

    const tasks = await Task.find(queryObj);

    res.status(200).json({
      status: 'success',
      results: tasks.length,
      data: {
        tasks // Wrap the array in a 'tasks' key
      }
```

```javascript
    });
  } catch (error) {
    // Pass errors to a centralized API error handler (similar to Chapter 4)
    next(error);
  }
};


// POST /api/v1/tasks - Create a new task
const createTask = async (req, res, next) => {
  try {
    // Data comes from req.body (assuming express.json() middleware is used)
    const newTask = await Task.create(req.body); // Shortcut for new Task() +
save()

    res.status(201).json({ // Use 201 Created status
      status: 'success',
      data: {
        task: newTask // Return the created task
      }
    });
  } catch (error) {
    // Handle Mongoose validation errors specifically for better client
feedback
    if (error.name === 'ValidationError') {
      const errors = Object.values(error.errors).map(el => el.message);
      const message = `Invalid input data. ${errors.join('. ')}`;
      // Ideally, create a reusable AppError class for structured errors
      // For now, send a 400 Bad Request
      return res.status(400).json({
        status: 'fail',
        message: message,
        errors: error.errors // Send detailed validation errors
      });
    }
    next(error); // Pass other errors on
  }
};


// GET /api/v1/tasks/:id - Get a single task
const getTaskById = async (req, res, next) => {
  try {
    const task = await Task.findById(req.params.id);

    if (!task) {
      // Use a consistent error response
      return res.status(404).json({
        status: 'fail',
```

```
          message: 'No task found with that ID'
      });
    }

    res.status(200).json({
      status: 'success',
      data: {
        task
      }
    });
  } catch (error) {
    next(error);
  }
};

// PATCH /api/v1/tasks/:id - Update a task (partial update)
const updateTask = async (req, res, next) => {
  try {
    const task = await Task.findByIdAndUpdate(req.params.id, req.body, {
      new: true, // Return the modified document rather than the original
      runValidators: true // Ensure updates adhere to schema validation
    });

    if (!task) {
      return res.status(404).json({
          status: 'fail',
          message: 'No task found with that ID'
        });
    }

    res.status(200).json({
      status: 'success',
      data: {
        task
      }
    });
  } catch (error) {
    // Handle validation errors on update
    if (error.name === 'ValidationError') {
      /* ... similar error handling as in createTask ... */
      return res.status(400).json({ /* ... */ });
    }
    next(error);
  }
};

// DELETE /api/v1/tasks/:id - Delete a task
```

```
const deleteTask = async (req, res, next) => {
  try {
    const task = await Task.findByIdAndDelete(req.params.id);

    if (!task) {
      return res.status(404).json({
          status: 'fail',
          message: 'No task found with that ID'
      });
    }

    // Send 204 No Content for successful deletion
    res.status(204).json({
      status: 'success',
      data: null // No data to send back
    });
  } catch (error) {
    next(error);
  }
};



module.exports = {
  getAllTasks,
  createTask,
  getTaskById,
  updateTask,
  deleteTask
};
```

3. Define Routes: Wire up the routes in routes/api/v1/tasks.js to use the controller functions.

```
// routes/api/v1/tasks.js
const express = require('express');
const taskApiController =
require('../../../controllers/api/v1/taskApiController'); // Adjust path
const router = express.Router();

// Define API routes
router.route('/')
  .get(taskApiController.getAllTasks)
  .post(taskApiController.createTask);

router.route('/:id')
  .get(taskApiController.getTaskById)
```

```
  .patch(taskApiController.updateTask) // Or .put() for full replacement
  .delete(taskApiController.deleteTask);

module.exports = router;
```

Using `router.route('/path')` *is a convenient way to chain handlers for different HTTP methods on the same path.*

4. Mount the API Router: In your main `app.js`, mount this API router under the `/api/v1` prefix.

```
// app.js
// ... (other setup, middleware like express.json()) ...

const taskApiRouter = require('./routes/api/v1/tasks'); // Adjust path

// Mount API router
app.use('/api/v1/tasks', taskApiRouter);

// --- API Error Handling ---
// Define a specific error handler for API routes
// It should come AFTER the API router is mounted.
app.use('/api', (err, req, res, next) => {
  // Log the error for debugging (consider more robust logging in production)
  console.error("API ERROR:", err.stack || err);

  // Set default status and message
  err.statusCode = err.statusCode || 500;
  err.status = err.status || 'error'; // 'fail' for client errors, 'error' for
server

  res.status(err.statusCode).json({
    status: err.status,
    message: err.message || 'Something went wrong!',
    // Optionally include stack trace in development environment
    // stack: process.env.NODE_ENV === 'development' ? err.stack : undefined
  });
});

// Note: You might also have a separate HTML error handler for non-API routes

// ... (app.listen) ...
```

Now you have a fully functional RESTful API for managing tasks! You can test it using tools like Postman, Insomnia, or `curl` to send GET, POST, PATCH, and DELETE requests with JSON data.

API Authentication (Brief Overview)

How do we protect these API endpoints? We can't rely on `express-session` and cookies like we did in Chapter 9. Why?

- **Statelessness:** REST APIs should be stateless. Relying on server-side sessions breaks this principle.
- **Non-Browser Clients:** Mobile apps or other servers consuming your API don't automatically manage cookies like browsers do.
- **Scalability:** Session stores can become bottlenecks in highly scaled API environments.

The standard approach for securing stateless APIs is **Token-Based Authentication**.

The Basic Flow:

1. **Login:** The client sends credentials (e.g., username/password) to a dedicated login endpoint (e.g., `POST /api/v1/auth/login`).
2. **Token Issuance:** The server validates the credentials. If valid, it generates a **token** (a string containing encoded information, often including user ID and an expiration time) and signs it cryptographically using a secret key known only to the server. **JSON Web Tokens (JWT)** are a very popular standard for these tokens.
3. **Token Delivery:** The server sends the generated token back to the client in the response body.
4. **Token Storage:** The client securely stores this token (e.g., in local storage for web apps, secure storage for mobile apps).
5. **Authenticated Requests:** For subsequent requests to protected API endpoints, the client includes the token in an HTTP header, typically the `Authorization` header using the `Bearer` scheme: `Authorization: Bearer <your_token_here>`.
6. **Token Verification:** On the server, middleware intercepts requests to protected endpoints. It extracts the token from the `Authorization` header, verifies its signature using the secret key, checks if it has expired, and potentially retrieves user information embedded within the token. If the token is valid, the middleware allows the request to proceed (often attaching user info to `req.user`); otherwise, it sends a `401 Unauthorized` error.

Other Mechanisms:

- **API Keys:** Simpler tokens often used for server-to-server communication or granting access to specific partners. The client includes the key in a header (e.g., X-API-Key: <your_key>) or query parameter. The server validates the key against a database. Less suitable for user-specific authentication.

Implementing full JWT authentication involves libraries like jsonwebtoken (npm install jsonwebtoken) for creating/verifying tokens and careful security considerations (like secure secret management, token expiration, refresh tokens). While a detailed implementation is beyond the scope of this chapter, understanding the token-based flow is essential when working with APIs. You would typically create middleware similar to requireLogin from Chapter 9, but instead of checking req.session.userId, it would verify the Authorization header token.

Chapter Summary

This chapter marked a shift from server-rendered applications to building **APIs**, specifically **RESTful APIs**, using Express. You learned that APIs act as contracts enabling communication between software components, often serving JSON data to clients like SPAs or mobile apps. We explored the core principles of **REST**, emphasizing **statelessness**, resource identification via URLs (using **nouns**), and leveraging standard **HTTP methods** (GET, POST, PUT, PATCH, DELETE) for actions.

We covered practical API design aspects like endpoint structure and the importance of **versioning** (/api/v1/...). You saw how to use res.json() to send standardized JSON responses with appropriate HTTP status codes and express.json() middleware to receive JSON data in req.body.

Crucially, you adapted the CRUD operations from previous chapters to create API endpoints for the Task resource, fetching data from Mongoose and responding with JSON. We organized these routes using express.Router and discussed creating dedicated API error handling middleware. Finally, we contrasted API authentication with session-based approaches, introducing the concept of **token-based authentication** (like JWT) as the standard for securing stateless APIs.

Your Express application is now capable of serving both traditional web pages and structured data via a well-designed API. But whether serving HTML or JSON, building robust applications requires attention to security. In the next chapter, we'll delve into common web security vulnerabilities and explore best practices and tools (like Helmet) to protect your Express applications and APIs from attack.

Chapter 11: Security Best Practices

Throughout our journey building web applications and APIs with Node.js and Express, we've focused on functionality: handling requests, managing routes, interacting with databases, handling forms, managing sessions, and even building APIs. But there's a critical aspect we haven't explicitly addressed yet, one that underpins the reliability and trustworthiness of any application: **security**. Security isn't a feature you sprinkle on at the end; it's a fundamental consideration that must be woven into every stage of development. A single vulnerability can compromise user data, damage your application's reputation, and lead to significant problems. In this chapter, we'll explore some of the most common web security threats relevant to Express applications and discuss practical best practices and tools to help you build more secure software.

Common Web Vulnerabilities

The web can be a dangerous place! Attackers constantly probe applications for weaknesses. Understanding common attack vectors is the first step towards defending against them. Here are some key vulnerabilities you should be aware of:

Cross-Site Scripting (XSS)
- **What it is:** XSS attacks occur when a malicious actor injects client-side scripts (usually JavaScript) into web pages viewed by other users. This script then executes within the victim's browser, potentially stealing session cookies (like the one used in Chapter 9), redirecting users to malicious sites, or defacing the website. This often happens when your application directly displays user-provided input without proper sanitization or escaping.
- **Prevention:**
  - **Output Escaping:** This is your **primary defense**. When rendering user-generated content in your HTML templates (Chapter 6), *always*

use the templating engine's escaping mechanism. In EJS, this is the `<%= ... %>` tag. It converts potentially harmful characters like `<` and `>` into harmless HTML entities (`&lt;`, `&gt;`), preventing the browser from interpreting them as code. Only use unescaped output (`<%- ... %>`) for content you absolutely trust (like including your own partials).

- **Input Validation/Sanitization:** Validate user input rigorously on the server-side (Chapter 8). While not a complete replacement for output escaping, sanitization techniques (like using `express-validator`'s `.escape()` or dedicated libraries to strip unwanted HTML) can provide an additional layer of defense by cleaning data *before* it's stored or processed.
- **Content Security Policy (CSP):** An HTTP header (`Content-Security-Policy`) that tells the browser which sources of content (scripts, styles, images) are allowed to be loaded and executed. A well-configured CSP can significantly mitigate the impact of XSS even if malicious script injection occurs. The `helmet` middleware (discussed later) helps set up CSP.

SQL Injection / NoSQL Injection

- **What it is:** Injection attacks happen when malicious input is crafted to manipulate database queries executed by your application. In SQL databases, attackers might inject partial SQL statements to bypass authentication, steal data, or delete records. Similar vulnerabilities exist in NoSQL databases (NoSQL Injection) if user input is directly concatenated into database query commands or operators without proper handling.
- **Prevention:**
    - **Use ORMs/ODMs Correctly:** Libraries like Mongoose (Chapter 7) provide a significant layer of protection against NoSQL injection *when used correctly*. Mongoose schemas define expected data types, and model methods (`.find()`, `.create()`, `.findByIdAndUpdate()`, etc.) typically handle input in a safer manner than manually constructing database commands. Avoid constructing MongoDB operators or query parts directly from raw user input.
    - **Parameterized Queries/Prepared Statements (SQL):** If working with SQL databases directly or through libraries that support it, always use parameterized queries or prepared statements. These mechanisms ensure that user input is treated strictly as data, not as executable code, by the database engine.

- **Input Validation:** Again, validate user input. Ensure IDs look like IDs, numbers are numbers, etc. This helps prevent malformed input from reaching the database layer.

Cross-Site Request Forgery (CSRF or XSRF)

- **What it is:** CSRF attacks trick a logged-in user's browser into making an unwanted request to your web application. Imagine a user is logged into your site (`my-app.com`). They then visit a malicious site (`evil.com`). `evil.com` could contain a hidden form or script that automatically submits a request to `my-app.com/transfer-funds` or `my-app.com/delete-account`. Since the user is logged into `my-app.com`, their browser automatically includes their session cookie (Chapter 9) with the request, making it look legitimate to your server. The user might perform a sensitive action without even knowing it.
- **Prevention:** The standard defense is using **CSRF Tokens**:
    1. When rendering a form that performs a state-changing action (POST, PUT, PATCH, DELETE), the server generates a unique, secret, unpredictable token associated with the user's session.
    2. This token is embedded as a hidden field within the form.
    3. When the form is submitted, the server checks if the submitted token matches the one stored in the user's session.
    4. If the tokens match, the request is valid. If they don't match (or the token is missing), the request is rejected, as it likely originated from a different source (like `evil.com`, which wouldn't know the secret token).
    5. **Middleware:** The `csurf` middleware (`npm install csurf`) is commonly used in Express to implement CSRF protection for session-based applications. You integrate it after the session and body-parsing middleware. It typically adds a token to `req.csrfToken()` which you then include in your forms, and it automatically verifies the token on subsequent state-changing requests.
    6. **Note:** CSRF is primarily a threat for **session-based authentication** where browsers automatically send cookies. It's generally less of a concern for **stateless, token-based APIs** (Chapter 10) where the client must explicitly include an `Authorization` header (which browsers don't send automatically across domains). Checking the `Origin` or `Referer` header can provide some additional defense, but CSRF tokens are more robust for session-based apps.

Insecure Direct Object References (IDOR)

- **What it is:** IDOR occurs when an application allows users to access resources (like documents, database records, files) based directly on user-supplied identifiers (like `/tasks/123`, `/invoices/90`, `/users/456/profile`) without properly checking if the *currently logged-in user* actually has permission to access *that specific resource*. An attacker might simply change the ID in the URL (`/tasks/124`, `/tasks/125`) to try and view or modify data belonging to other users.
- **Prevention: Authorization Checks!** This ties directly into the authentication and authorization middleware discussed in Chapter 9. It's not enough to just check *if* a user is logged in (`requireLogin`). For any route that accesses a specific resource by ID, you **must** verify that the resource actually belongs to, or is accessible by, the currently authenticated user.
    - Example: When handling `PATCH /tasks/:id`, fetch the task *and* check if `task.ownerId` (assuming you store who owns the task) matches `req.session.userId` (or `req.user.id` if using token auth) before allowing the update. If they don't match, return a `403 Forbidden` or `404 Not Found` status.

Security Misconfiguration

- **What it is:** This is a broad category covering various setup and configuration mistakes:
    - Using default usernames/passwords for databases or admin accounts.
    - Leaving debugging modes or verbose error messages enabled in production (leaking stack traces or internal information).
    - Running outdated software (Node.js, Express, databases, libraries) with known vulnerabilities.
    - Improper file and directory permissions on the server.
    - Not configuring necessary security headers.
- **Prevention:**
    - Change all default credentials immediately.
    - Configure proper error handling that logs details server-side but shows generic error messages to users in production (use `process.env.NODE_ENV === 'production'` checks).
    - Keep all software components up-to-date (see "Keeping Dependencies Updated" below).
    - Follow least privilege principles for server configurations.
    - Use security header middleware like `helmet`.

Security Headers with `helmet`

HTTP headers are a powerful way to instruct the browser on how to behave regarding security. Manually setting all the recommended headers can be tedious. The `helmet` middleware simplifies this greatly. It's a collection of smaller middleware functions that set various security-related HTTP headers.

1. **Install**: `npm install helmet --save`

2. **Use**: Apply it as application-level middleware, preferably early in your middleware stack.

```
// app.js
const express = require('express');
const helmet = require('helmet'); // Import helmet
const app = express();

// Use helmet middleware
// It sets various headers like CSP, X-Frame-Options, HSTS, etc.
app.use(helmet());

// If you need to configure specific headers set by helmet,
// you can pass options or use individual helmet sub-middleware.
// Example: Setting a basic Content Security Policy (CSP)
// app.use(helmet.contentSecurityPolicy({
//    directives: {
//      defaultSrc: ["'self'"], // Only allow resources from same origin
//      scriptSrc: ["'self'", 'trusted-cdn.com'], // Allow scripts from
self and trusted CDN
//      // ... other directives (styleSrc, imgSrc, etc.)
//    }
// }));

// ... (rest of your app setup) ...
```

By default, `helmet()` enables a sensible set of security headers, including:

- `Content-Security-Policy` (CSP): Helps prevent XSS by defining allowed sources for content. (Highly configurable).
- `Strict-Transport-Security` (HSTS): Tells browsers to only communicate with your server over HTTPS.
- `X-Content-Type-Options`: Prevents browsers from MIME-sniffing response types.
- `X-DNS-Prefetch-Control`: Controls browser DNS prefetching.

117

- `X-Download-Options`: Helps prevent execution of downloads in IE.
- `X-Frame-Options`: Prevents your pages from being embedded in iframes on other sites (clickjacking defense).
- `X-Permitted-Cross-Domain-Policies`: Restricts Adobe Flash/PDF access to data.
- `X-XSS-Protection`: Enables the XSS filter built into most browsers (though largely superseded by CSP).
- And others... Refer to the `helmet` documentation for the full list and configuration options. Using `helmet` is a simple and effective way to improve your application's baseline security posture.

HTTPS

Using **HTTPS (HTTP Secure)** is non-negotiable for any application that handles sensitive data (like logins, personal information, or financial transactions). HTTP sends data in plain text, making it vulnerable to eavesdropping and modification. HTTPS encrypts the communication between the client's browser and your server using TLS/SSL protocols.

- **Why it's essential:**
    - **Encryption:** Protects data confidentiality.
    - **Integrity:** Ensures data hasn't been tampered with in transit.
    - **Authentication:** Helps verify that the client is talking to the real server (preventing man-in-the-middle attacks).
    - **Browser Trust:** Browsers increasingly flag HTTP sites as "Not Secure."
    - **Required for Features:** Many modern browser features (like Geolocation, Service Workers) require HTTPS.
- **Obtaining Certificates:** You need an SSL/TLS certificate issued by a trusted Certificate Authority (CA). **Let's Encrypt** is a free, automated, and open CA that makes obtaining certificates easy. Many hosting providers offer integrated Let's Encrypt support.
- **Configuration:** While Node.js's built-in `https` module can be used to create an HTTPS server directly, in production environments, it's very common to handle HTTPS termination at a **reverse proxy** level (like Nginx or Apache) or using a load balancer. The reverse proxy handles the SSL/TLS handshake and forwards decrypted traffic to your Node.js/Express application running on a standard HTTP port locally on the server. This simplifies your Node.js configuration and often provides better performance for SSL handling. Your hosting provider's documentation will usually guide you on setting up HTTPS.

Rate Limiting

Imagine an attacker trying to guess user passwords by rapidly submitting login requests (a brute-force attack) or simply overwhelming your server by sending thousands of requests per second (Denial-of-Service - DoS). **Rate limiting** helps mitigate these threats by restricting the number of requests a client (identified by IP address or other means) can make within a certain time window.

The `express-rate-limit` middleware is a popular choice for implementing this:

1. **Install:** `npm install express-rate-limit --save`
2. **Configure and Use:** Apply it globally or specifically to sensitive endpoints (like login or API routes).

```
// app.js
const rateLimit = require('express-rate-limit');

// Apply rate limiting to all requests
// (Adjust settings based on your application's needs)
const limiter = rateLimit({
  windowMs: 15 * 60 * 1000, // 15 minutes window
  max: 100, // Limit each IP to 100 requests per windowMs
  message: 'Too many requests from this IP, please try again after 15 minutes',
  standardHeaders: true, // Return rate limit info in the `RateLimit-*` headers
  legacyHeaders: false, // Disable the `X-RateLimit-*` headers
});
app.use(limiter);

// You might apply stricter limits specifically to authentication routes:
const authLimiter = rateLimit({
  windowMs: 60 * 60 * 1000, // 1 hour window
  max: 5, // Limit each IP to 5 login attempts per hour
  message: 'Too many login attempts from this IP, please try again after an
hour',
  // skipSuccessfulRequests: true // Optionally skip successful auth requests
});
// Assuming you have an authRouter mounted at /auth
app.use('/auth/login', authLimiter); // Apply specifically to login POST route

// ... (rest of app setup) ...
```

Adjust the `windowMs` and `max` values based on your expected traffic and the sensitivity of the endpoints.

Keeping Dependencies Updated

Your application relies not only on Node.js and Express but also on numerous third-party packages installed via npm (Mongoose, EJS, Helmet, session stores, etc.). These packages can, and often do, have security vulnerabilities discovered over time. Running outdated dependencies is a significant security risk.

- `npm audit`: This command checks your project's dependencies against the npm registry's database of known vulnerabilities. Run it periodically:

  ```
  npm audit
  ```

  It will report vulnerabilities found and often suggest commands (`npm audit fix`) to update packages to patched versions automatically (though manual review is sometimes needed for major version bumps).
- **Regular Updates:** Make it a practice to regularly update your dependencies to their latest stable versions (`npm update`). While potentially introducing breaking changes that require testing, staying current is crucial for security. Services like GitHub's Dependabot can automate the process of creating pull requests for dependency updates.

Chapter Summary

Security is an ongoing process, not a one-time task. In this chapter, we highlighted its importance and explored several critical web vulnerabilities: Cross-Site Scripting (XSS), SQL/NoSQL Injection, Cross-Site Request Forgery (CSRF), and Insecure Direct Object References (IDOR), along with general Security Misconfigurations. For each, we discussed the threat and key prevention strategies relevant to Express applications, reinforcing concepts like output escaping, correct ORM/ODM usage, CSRF tokens, and diligent authorization checks.

You learned how the `helmet` middleware provides an easy way to set crucial security-related HTTP headers, enhancing your application's defenses. We underscored the necessity of using HTTPS for encrypted communication and touched upon certificate acquisition and common production setups involving reverse proxies. We also addressed mitigating brute-force and DoS attacks using rate limiting with `express-rate-limit`. Finally, we emphasized the vital importance of keeping your Node.js environment and all npm dependencies up-to-date using tools like `npm audit` to patch known vulnerabilities.

Building secure applications requires vigilance at every step. While we've covered key practices, security is a deep field. Always keep learning and stay aware of emerging threats. Now that you have a better understanding of how to build functional *and* more secure applications, how do you ensure they actually work as intended and continue to work after making changes? In the next chapter, we'll introduce **testing** strategies for your Express applications, helping you build confidence in your code's correctness and stability.

Chapter 12: Testing Your Application

You've diligently built your Express application, carefully crafting routes, connecting to databases, handling user input, implementing security measures, and perhaps even building APIs. It works... on your machine, when you test it manually. But how can you be *sure* it works correctly under various conditions? How do you prevent accidentally breaking existing features when you add new ones or refactor code? Manually testing every part of your application after every change is time-consuming, tedious, and prone to human error. This is where **automated testing** becomes an indispensable part of the development process. Writing tests might seem like extra work initially, but it pays off immensely in the long run by providing confidence, stability, and maintainability for your project. Let's explore how to start testing your Express applications.

Why Test?

Before diving into the "how," let's solidify the "why." Why invest time writing code that tests your *other* code?

- **Confidence:** Automated tests act as a safety net. When tests pass, you have greater confidence that your code behaves as expected and that recent changes haven't broken anything crucial. This confidence speeds up development because you're less afraid to make changes or refactor.
- **Catching Bugs Early (Regression Prevention):** Tests help catch bugs much earlier in the development cycle, often immediately after they are introduced. This is far cheaper and easier than fixing bugs discovered much later by users in production. Tests prevent *regressions* – bugs that reappear after having been fixed previously.

- **Documentation:** Well-written tests serve as living documentation for your code. They demonstrate exactly how specific functions or API endpoints are intended to be used and what outputs are expected for given inputs.
- **Maintainability and Refactoring:** When you have a solid test suite, refactoring code (improving its structure without changing its external behavior) becomes much less daunting. You can restructure your controllers, models, or helper functions, and as long as the tests still pass, you know you haven't broken the core functionality.
- **Collaboration:** Tests provide a shared understanding of how the code should work, making it easier for teams to collaborate and for new developers to get up to speed.

Think of testing like having safety checks for building a bridge. You wouldn't just build it and hope it holds; you'd perform stress tests and measurements at various stages to ensure it's sound. Automated tests do the same for your software.

Types of Tests (Brief Overview)

Testing exists on different levels of granularity. While the lines can sometimes blur, understanding these categories is helpful:

- **Unit Tests:** These tests focus on the smallest testable parts of your application, typically individual functions or modules, in **isolation**. If a function relies on other parts (like a database or another module), those dependencies are usually "mocked" or "stubbed" – replaced with fake versions that return predictable results. This ensures you're testing *only* the logic within that specific unit.
  - *Example:* Testing a helper function that formats dates, or testing a specific calculation within a controller method (mocking any database calls it makes).
- **Integration Tests:** These tests verify that different parts (units or modules) of your application work correctly *together*. For Express applications, this often means testing a complete request-response cycle: making an HTTP request to a specific route and checking if the route handler, controller, and potentially database interaction produce the expected outcome (like the correct HTTP status code, response body, or database state). Dependencies like the database might be real (using a dedicated test database) or mocked, depending on the specific test goal.
  - *Example:* Testing if a POST request to `/api/v1/tasks` actually creates a task in the test database and returns a `201 Created` status with the correct JSON response.

- **End-to-End (E2E) Tests:** These tests simulate a real user interacting with the entire application, usually through a browser interface. They verify complete workflows from start to finish (e.g., logging in, navigating to a page, filling out a form, submitting it, and verifying the result on the page). E2E tests provide the highest level of confidence but are also the slowest and most brittle (prone to breaking due to UI changes). Tools like Cypress or Playwright are commonly used for E2E testing.
  - *Example:* Automating a browser to visit `/login`, enter credentials, navigate to `/tasks/new`, fill the task form, submit, and verify the new task appears in the list on the `/tasks` page.

For backend development with Express, **integration tests** often provide the most value, as they verify that your routes, middleware, controllers, and data layers work together as intended. Unit tests are also valuable for isolating complex logic within helper functions or specific controller methods. We'll focus primarily on unit and integration testing in this chapter.

Testing Tools

The Node.js ecosystem offers a rich set of tools for testing. Here are the ones we'll use:

- **Test Runner:** A program that discovers, executes, and reports the results of your tests.
  - **Mocha:** A flexible, popular, and widely used JavaScript test framework. It provides the basic structure for organizing tests (`describe`, `it`) and running them. We'll use Mocha. (Alternatives: Jest, Jasmine).
- **Assertion Library:** A library that provides functions to verify that expectations in your tests are met. Assertions check if a value is what you expect it to be (e.g., equal to another value, true, not null).
  - **Chai:** A highly expressive assertion library that works well with Mocha. It offers several "styles" of assertions (like `expect`, `should`, `assert`). We'll primarily use the `expect` style. (Alternatives: Node's built-in `assert` module, Jest's built-in matchers).
- **HTTP Request Library for Testing:** For integration testing Express routes, we need a way to make HTTP requests to our application *within* our test code and assert the responses.
  - **Supertest:** Specifically designed for testing Node.js HTTP servers. It allows you to programmatically send requests to your Express `app` object without needing to run the server on an actual network port,

making tests faster and more reliable. It integrates beautifully with Mocha and Chai.

Setting up a Test Environment

Let's get our testing tools installed and configured.

1. **Install Development Dependencies:** Testing tools are usually needed only during development, not in production. We install them as "dev dependencies" using the --save-dev flag (or -D). Open your terminal in your project directory (my-express-app) and run:

```
npm install --save-dev mocha chai supertest
# Or: npm install -D mocha chai supertest
```

This adds mocha, chai, and supertest to the devDependencies section of your package.json.

2. **Create a Test Script in** package.json: Add a script to your package.json file to easily run your tests using Mocha.

```
// package.json
{
  // ... other properties (name, version, dependencies, etc.)
  "scripts": {
    "start": "node app.js", // Your existing start script
    "dev": "nodemon app.js", // Optional: if using nodemon
    "test": "mocha" // Add this line
    // You can add options, e.g., "mocha test/**/*.test.js" to specify
files
  },
  // ... (devDependencies, etc.)
}
```

Now you can run all your tests from the terminal using the command: npm test. Mocha will automatically look for tests (by default in a test directory).

3. **Organize Test Files:** Create a directory named test in the root of your project. This is the conventional place to keep your test files. Inside test, you might further structure tests based on what they are testing (e.g., test/utils.test.js, test/tasks.api.test.js). Test files often use .test.js or .spec.js extensions.

4. **Test Environment Considerations:**

- **Environment Variable:** It's common practice to set `NODE_ENV=test` when running tests. This allows your application code (e.g., in database connection logic or error handlers) to behave differently during testing if needed (like connecting to a test database or showing more detailed errors). You can set this variable when running the test script:

```
// package.json (example using cross-env for cross-platform
compatibility)
// First run: npm install --save-dev cross-env
"scripts": {
  // ...
    "test": "cross-env NODE_ENV=test mocha"
},
```

- **Test Database:** For integration tests involving database interactions, **do not run tests against your development or production database!** You risk polluting or deleting real data. Use a separate database instance dedicated solely for testing. We'll discuss strategies for managing this later.

Writing Unit Tests

Let's start with a simple unit test. Imagine you have a helper function in a file `utils/formatters.js` that formats a date object.

```
// utils/formatters.js
const formatDate = (date) => {
  if (!(date instanceof Date) || isNaN(date)) {
    return 'Invalid Date';
  }
  // Simple YYYY-MM-DD format
  const year = date.getFullYear();
  const month = String(date.getMonth() + 1).padStart(2, '0'); // Month is 0-
indexed
  const day = String(date.getDate()).padStart(2, '0');
  return `${year}-${month}-${day}`;
};

module.exports = { formatDate };
```

Now, let's write a test for this function. Create `test/formatters.test.js`:

```javascript
// test/formatters.test.js
const { expect } = require('chai'); // Import expect style from Chai
const { formatDate } = require('../utils/formatters'); // Import the function to
test

// Use Mocha's 'describe' to group related tests
describe('Utils - Formatters', () => {

  // Describe the specific function being tested
  describe('formatDate()', () => {

    // Use Mocha's 'it' to define an individual test case
    it('should return date in YYYY-MM-DD format for valid Date object', () => {
      const date = new Date(2023, 9, 28); // Note: Month is 0-indexed (9 =
October)
      const expectedOutput = '2023-10-28';
      const actualOutput = formatDate(date);

      // Use Chai's 'expect' to make an assertion
      expect(actualOutput).to.equal(expectedOutput);
    });

    it('should handle single digit month and day with padding', () => {
      const date = new Date(2024, 0, 5); // January 5th
      const expectedOutput = '2024-01-05';
      const actualOutput = formatDate(date);
      expect(actualOutput).to.equal(expectedOutput);
    });

    it('should return "Invalid Date" for non-Date input', () => {
      expect(formatDate('2023-10-28')).to.equal('Invalid Date');
      expect(formatDate(null)).to.equal('Invalid Date');
      expect(formatDate({})).to.equal('Invalid Date');
    });

    it('should return "Invalid Date" for invalid Date object', () => {
      const invalidDate = new Date('not a real date');
      expect(formatDate(invalidDate)).to.equal('Invalid Date');
    });

  }); // End describe formatDate()

  // You could add describe blocks for other functions in formatters.js here

}); // End describe Utils - Formatters
```

Explanation:

127

- `require('chai').expect`: Imports the expect assertion style.
- `require('../utils/formatters')`: Imports the actual code we want to test.
- `describe('Group Name', () => { ... });`: Mocha function to group related tests. You can nest `describe` blocks.
- `it('should do something specific', () => { ... });`: Mocha function defining an individual test case. The string describes what the test should verify.
- `expect(actualValue).to.equal(expectedValue);`: A Chai assertion. It checks if `actualValue` is strictly equal to `expectedValue`. If not, the test fails. Chai offers many other assertions (`.to.be.true`, `.to.include()`, `.to.be.an('object')`, etc.).

Run `npm test` in your terminal. Mocha should find and run this test file, reporting the results (hopefully passing!).

Writing Integration Tests with Supertest

Now for the core of backend testing: integration tests for our Express routes. Let's test the Task API endpoints we created in Chapter 10 (`/api/v1/tasks`).

We need access to our configured Express app instance within the test file. A common pattern is to export the app from `app.js` *without* calling `app.listen()` directly in that file. Create a separate `server.js` file that imports app and calls `listen`.

Refactor `app.js` (Example):

```
// app.js
const express = require('express');
const helmet = require('helmet');
const path = require('path');
const session = require('express-session'); // If using sessions
// ... other requires (dotenv, mongoose, connect-mongo, connect-flash)

// Database connection (ensure this runs)
// require('./config/db')(); // Or however you connect

const app = express(); // Create app instance

// --- View Engine / Middleware ---
app.set('view engine', 'ejs');
app.set('views', path.join(__dirname, 'views'));

app.use(helmet());
```

```
app.use(express.json()); // For API JSON bodies
app.use(express.urlencoded({ extended: true })); // For form bodies
app.use(express.static(path.join(__dirname, 'public')));

// Session & Flash (if needed for parts of your app)
// app.use(session({...}));
// app.use(flash());
// app.use((req, res, next) => { ... }); // Flash message middleware

// --- Routers ---
// Example: HTML routes
// const indexRouter = require('./routes/index');
// app.use('/', indexRouter);

// API routes
const taskApiRouter = require('./routes/api/v1/tasks'); // Adjust path
app.use('/api/v1/tasks', taskApiRouter);

// --- Error Handlers ---
// API Error Handler
app.use('/api', (err, req, res, next) => { /* ... API error handler ... */ });
// HTML Error Handler
app.use((err, req, res, next) => { /* ... HTML error handler ... */ });

// --- Export the app ---
// DO NOT call app.listen() here
module.exports = app;
```

Create server.js:

```
// server.js
const app = require('./app'); // Import the configured app

const port = process.env.PORT || 3000;

// Start the server by listening
app.listen(port, () => {
  console.log(`Server listening on port ${port}...`);
});
```

Now, your normal start script (npm start or npm run dev) should run node server-
.js. But your tests can require('./app') to get the configured Express app object
without actually starting the server listener.

Create test/tasks.api.test.js:

129

```javascript
// test/tasks.api.test.js
const request = require('supertest'); // Import supertest
const { expect } = require('chai');
const app = require('../app'); // Import your configured Express app
const Task = require('../models/Task'); // Import Task model for setup/teardown

describe('API - Tasks Routes (/api/v1/tasks)', () => {

  // --- Test Hooks ---
  // Optional: Run code before/after tests using hooks like
  // before(), after(), beforeEach(), afterEach()

  // Example: Clear the Task collection before each test
  beforeEach(async () => {
    // Connect to test DB if not already connected (handle elsewhere ideally)
    // Clear the collection
    try {
      await Task.deleteMany({}); // Delete all tasks
      console.log('Test DB: Tasks collection cleared.');
    } catch (error) {
      console.error("Error clearing test DB:", error);
      // Handle connection errors if necessary
      throw error; // Fail tests if DB cleanup fails
    }
  });

  // --- GET /api/v1/tasks ---
  describe('GET /', () => {
    it('should return an empty array when no tasks exist', async () => {
      const res = await request(app)
        .get('/api/v1/tasks')
        .expect('Content-Type', /json/) // Check Content-Type header
        .expect(200); // Check status code

      // Use Chai to assert the response body structure and content
      expect(res.body).to.be.an('object');
      expect(res.body.status).to.equal('success');
      expect(res.body.results).to.equal(0);
      expect(res.body.data).to.be.an('object');
      expect(res.body.data.tasks).to.be.an('array').that.is.empty;
    });

    it('should return all tasks when tasks exist', async () => {
      // Seed the database with some test data
      await Task.insertMany([
        { description: 'Test Task 1' },
        { description: 'Test Task 2', completed: true }
```

```
      ]);

      const res = await request(app)
        .get('/api/v1/tasks')
        .expect(200);

      expect(res.body.status).to.equal('success');
      expect(res.body.results).to.equal(2);
      expect(res.body.data.tasks).to.be.an('array').with.lengthOf(2);
      expect(res.body.data.tasks[0].description).to.equal('Test Task 1');
      expect(res.body.data.tasks[1].completed).to.be.true;
    });
  }); // End GET /

  // --- POST /api/v1/tasks ---
  describe('POST /', () => {
    it('should create a new task with valid data', async () => {
      const newTaskData = { description: 'New API Task' };

      const res = await request(app)
        .post('/api/v1/tasks')
        .send(newTaskData) // Send data in request body
        .expect('Content-Type', /json/)
        .expect(201); // Expect 201 Created status

      expect(res.body.status).to.equal('success');
      expect(res.body.data).to.be.an('object');
      expect(res.body.data.task).to.be.an('object');
      expect(res.body.data.task.description).to.equal(newTaskData.description);
      expect(res.body.data.task.completed).to.be.false; // Check default value
      expect(res.body.data.task._id).to.be.a('string'); // Check if ID was
generated

      // Optional: Verify task was actually saved in the DB
      const taskInDb = await Task.findById(res.body.data.task._id);
      expect(taskInDb).to.not.be.null;
      expect(taskInDb.description).to.equal(newTaskData.description);
    });

    it('should return 400 Bad Request for invalid data (missing description)',
async () => {
      const invalidData = { completed: true }; // Missing description

      const res = await request(app)
        .post('/api/v1/tasks')
        .send(invalidData)
        .expect('Content-Type', /json/)
```

```
            .expect(400);

        expect(res.body.status).to.equal('fail');
        expect(res.body.message).to.include('Invalid input data.');
        // Check specific validation errors if your handler provides them
         expect(res.body.errors).to.be.an('object');
         expect(res.body.errors.description.message).to.equal('Task description
cannot be empty');
    });
  }); // End POST /

  // --- GET /api/v1/tasks/:id ---
  describe('GET /:id', () => {
    it('should return a single task if ID is valid and exists', async () => {
        const task = await new Task({ description: 'Find Me' }).save();
        const taskId = task._id;

        const res = await request(app)
            .get(`/api/v1/tasks/${taskId}`)
            .expect(200);

        expect(res.body.status).to.equal('success');
        expect(res.body.data.task._id).to.equal(String(taskId));
        expect(res.body.data.task.description).to.equal('Find Me');
    });

    it('should return 404 Not Found if ID is valid but does not exist', async
() => {
        const nonExistentId = new mongoose.Types.ObjectId(); // Generate valid
ObjectId
        const res = await request(app)
            .get(`/api/v1/tasks/${nonExistentId}`)
            .expect(404);

        expect(res.body.status).to.equal('fail');
        expect(res.body.message).to.equal('No task found with that ID');
    });

    it('should return 500 Internal Server Error (or similar) if ID is
invalid', async () => {
        // Mongoose might throw CastError for invalid ID format before
controller check
        const invalidId = 'this-is-not-a-valid-id';
        const res = await request(app)
            .get(`/api/v1/tasks/${invalidId}`)
            .expect(500); // Or potentially 400 depending on error handling
```

```
            // Check error structure based on your API error handler
            expect(res.body.status).to.equal('error'); // Or 'fail'
            // Add more specific checks if needed
        });
    }); // End GET /:id

    // --- Add tests for PATCH /:id and DELETE /:id similarly ---

}); // End describe API - Tasks Routes
```

Explanation:

- `request(app)`: Creates a Supertest request agent using your Express app.
- `.get('/path')`, `.post('/path')`, **etc.:** Chain HTTP methods to specify the request.
- `.send(data)`: Sends data in the request body (for POST, PUT, PATCH). Supertest automatically sets `Content-Type` to `application/json` if you send an object.
- `.expect(statusCode)`: Asserts the HTTP status code of the response.
- `.expect('Header-Name', /value_pattern/)`: Asserts the value of a response header (can use strings or regex).
- `.expect(callback)`: Allows more complex assertions on the response body using a callback function.
- `async/await`: Supertest methods return Promises, so we use `async/await` to write asynchronous tests cleanly. Mocha automatically handles Promises returned by `it` blocks.
- **Hooks** (`beforeEach`, `afterEach`): Mocha provides hooks to run setup/teardown code before/after all tests (`before/after`) or before/after each individual test (`beforeEach/afterEach`). These are essential for managing test environments, especially when interacting with a database.

Handling Asynchronous Operations

As seen in the Supertest example, most integration tests involving network requests or database operations will be asynchronous.

- Use async keyword before your `it` callback function: `it('should ...', async () => { ... });`.
- Use `await` when calling asynchronous functions (like Supertest request methods or Mongoose operations).

- Mocha will automatically wait for the Promise returned by the `async` function to resolve or reject before considering the test finished.

Database Interaction in Tests

Testing code that interacts with a database requires careful consideration. As mentioned, never test against your production database. Common strategies include:

1. **Using a Test Database:**

   - Set up a separate database instance (e.g., a different MongoDB database like `myExpressAppDB_Test`) specifically for running tests.
   - Configure your application (perhaps using `process.env.NODE_ENV === 'test'`) to connect to this test database when tests are run.
   - Use test hooks (`beforeEach` or `afterEach`) to ensure the database is in a clean, known state before each test runs (e.g., `Task.deleteMany({})` to clear the tasks collection).
   - **Pros:** Tests run against a real database, providing higher confidence that database interactions work correctly.
   - **Cons:** Slower than mocking, requires database setup and management.

2. **Mocking/Stubbing the Database Layer:**

   - Use libraries like `sinon` or Jest's built-in mocking capabilities to replace your Mongoose models or database interaction functions with fake versions ("mocks" or "stubs") during tests.
   - These mocks return predefined data, allowing you to test your controller/route logic without actually hitting the database.
   - **Pros:** Faster tests, tests are truly isolated.
   - **Cons:** Can be complex to set up mocks correctly, tests don't verify actual database interactions.

For integration tests of Express routes, using a **real test database** is often the preferred approach as it more accurately reflects how the application components work together. Ensure your database connection logic checks `process.env.NODE_ENV` and connects appropriately.

Chapter Summary

In this chapter, you learned the critical importance of automated testing for building reliable and maintainable Express applications. We discussed the key benefits:

increased confidence, early bug detection (regression prevention), documentation, and safer refactoring. You got an overview of different test types (Unit, Integration, E2E), focusing on the value of unit and integration tests for backend development.

We introduced the essential testing toolkit: **Mocha** as the test runner, **Chai** for expressive assertions (expect), and **Supertest** for making HTTP requests to your Express app within tests. You learned how to set up your environment by installing dev dependencies and configuring an npm test script.

We walked through practical examples of writing **unit tests** for helper functions and, more importantly, **integration tests** for your API routes using Supertest. You saw how to make requests, assert status codes, headers, and response bodies, and handle asynchronous operations using async/await. We also covered the crucial aspect of managing database interactions during testing, highlighting the common strategy of using a dedicated **test database** and employing test hooks (beforeEach) for cleanup.

Writing tests might take some extra effort upfront, but the long-term benefits in stability and development speed are substantial. With a tested application, you're now much better prepared for the final step: getting your application online for the world to use. In the next chapter, we'll explore various **deployment strategies**, taking your tested Node.js and Express application from your local machine to a live production server.

Chapter 13: Deployment Strategies

You've successfully navigated the world of Node.js and Express, building features, securing endpoints, writing tests, and interacting with databases. Your application runs smoothly on your local machine. But the ultimate goal is usually to share your creation with the world, making it accessible to users over the internet. This final step involves **deployment** – the process of taking your application code and putting it onto a server infrastructure where it can run reliably and handle real user traffic. Transitioning from the controlled environment of your laptop to a live production server involves several important considerations and choices. Let's explore the common strategies for deploying your Node.js and Express application.

Preparing for Production

Before you even think about pushing your code to a live server, there are several crucial preparatory steps to ensure a smoother and more secure deployment. The production environment has different requirements than your development setup.

Environment Variables (`NODE_ENV=production`)

This is perhaps the single most important configuration setting. You should always set the `NODE_ENV` environment variable to the literal string `production` on your live servers. Many libraries, including Express itself, check this variable and alter their behavior accordingly:

- **Performance:** Express enables view caching and other optimizations when `NODE_ENV` is `production`.
- **Error Handling:** Verbose error messages and stack traces, helpful during development, should *never* be shown to end-users in production as they can leak sensitive information. Frameworks and your own error handling logic

(Chapter 11) should check `process.env.NODE_ENV` and provide generic error responses in production.

- **Logging:** You might configure more detailed logging in development but less verbose (or differently formatted) logging in production.
- **Dependency Installation:** Running `npm install --production` (or having `NODE_ENV=production` set when running `npm install`) skips installing packages listed in your `devDependencies` (like Mocha, Chai, Nodemon), keeping your production deployment leaner.

While we used the `dotenv` package (Chapter 7) to load variables from a `.env` file for convenience in *development*, you typically **do not deploy the `.env` file itself** to production. Instead, you set the *actual* environment variables directly on the hosting platform or server where your application will run. This includes `NODE_ENV=production`, your `DATABASE_URI`, `SESSION_SECRET`, any API keys, and other configuration secrets.

Configuration Management

Stemming from environment variables, ensure your application correctly handles different configurations between environments. Hardcoding database connection strings or API keys directly in your code is a major security risk and makes switching environments difficult. Always fetch configuration values from `process.env`.

Logging

Relying solely on `console.log()` in production is insufficient. If your application crashes or encounters issues, those logs might be lost or difficult to access and parse. Use a dedicated, robust logging library designed for production use. Popular choices include:

- **Winston:** A highly configurable and popular logging library.
- **Pino:** Known for extremely high performance and structured JSON logging.

These libraries allow you to:

- Define different **logging levels** (e.g., `error`, `warn`, `info`, `debug`). You typically log at `info` or `warn` level in production, saving `debug` for troubleshooting.
- Output logs in a **structured format** (like JSON), making them easier to parse by log analysis tools (e.g., ELK stack, Datadog, Splunk).
- Direct logs to various **transports** (e.g., console, files, remote logging services).

Configure your chosen logger early in your application setup (`app.js`).

Error Handling

Revisit your error handling middleware (Chapters 4 and 11). Ensure that in production (`process.env.NODE_ENV === 'production'`), you log detailed error information (including stack traces) server-side but send only generic, user-friendly error messages or pages to the client. Never leak internal implementation details or stack traces in production responses.

Deployment Options Overview

Where can you actually host your Node.js application? There are several categories of hosting solutions, each with trade-offs:

Platform as a Service (PaaS)

- **Concept:** You provide your application code, and the PaaS provider manages the underlying infrastructure – servers, operating systems, patching, networking, scaling infrastructure (often). You interact through a web dashboard or command-line tools.
- **Examples:** Heroku, Render, Vercel (especially good for frontend + Node API), DigitalOcean App Platform, Google App Engine, AWS Elastic Beanstalk.
- **Pros:**
    - **Ease of Use:** Significantly simplifies deployment. Often integrates directly with Git repositories (like GitHub, GitLab).
    - **Faster Setup:** You can get an application running quickly without managing servers directly.
    - **Scalability Features:** Many PaaS providers offer easy scaling (adding more instances or resources) via sliders or configuration.
    - **Managed Services:** Often include easy integration with databases, caching, etc.
- **Cons:**
    - **Less Control:** You have limited access to the underlying operating system or server configuration.
    - **Potential Vendor Lock-in:** Migrating away from a specific PaaS can sometimes be complex.
    - **Cost:** Can become more expensive than managing your own servers at larger scales or with high resource usage, although many offer generous free/hobby tiers to start.

PaaS is an excellent choice for startups, side projects, and teams that want to focus on application development rather than infrastructure management.

Infrastructure as a Service (IaaS) / Virtual Private Servers (VPS)

- **Concept:** You rent virtual machines (servers) from a cloud provider. You get root access and are responsible for installing the operating system (usually chosen from templates), configuring the network, installing Node.js, setting up the database (or connecting to a managed one), managing security, and deploying your code.
- **Examples:** DigitalOcean Droplets, Linode, AWS EC2, Google Compute Engine, Azure Virtual Machines.
- **Pros:**
    - **Full Control:** Complete flexibility over the server environment, software installations, and configuration.
    - **Cost-Effective (Potentially):** Often cheaper than PaaS for consistent, predictable workloads, especially at scale.
    - **No Vendor Lock-in (at OS level):** Easier to migrate between IaaS providers if needed.
- **Cons:**
    - **Requires Server Management:** You are responsible for setup, maintenance, security patching, backups, monitoring, etc.
    - **Steeper Learning Curve:** Requires system administration knowledge.
    - **Manual Scaling:** Scaling usually involves manually provisioning more servers and configuring load balancing.

VPS/IaaS is suitable when you need fine-grained control over the environment, have specific software requirements not met by PaaS, or have the resources and expertise for server management.

Containers (Docker / Kubernetes)

- **Concept:** You package your application and all its dependencies (Node.js runtime, libraries) into a standardized unit called a **container** (using tools like **Docker**). This container can then run consistently across different environments (developer machine, testing server, production). **Kubernetes** is a popular orchestration platform used to manage, scale, and deploy containerized applications across clusters of servers.
- **Pros:** Consistency across environments, simplified dependency management, excellent scalability, ecosystem of tools.
- **Cons:** Adds another layer of abstraction, learning curve for Docker and especially Kubernetes can be significant.

Containerization is increasingly popular, especially for microservices and large-scale applications, but often represents a more advanced deployment strategy.

Simple PaaS Deployment Example (Render)

Let's walk through deploying our Express app using Render, a popular PaaS provider known for its ease of use and free tier suitable for small projects. The process is similar for other providers like Heroku.

Prerequisites:

1. Your application code is in a Git repository (e.g., on GitHub, GitLab, Bitbucket).

2. Your application listens on the port specified by the PORT environment variable (provided by the platform). Modify your server.js (or wherever you call app.listen):

```
// server.js
const app = require('./app');
// Render (and most PaaS) sets the PORT environment variable
const port = process.env.PORT || 3000; // Use PaaS port or default to
3000
app.listen(port, () => {
    console.log(`Server listening on port ${port}...`);
});
```

3. Ensure your package.json has a correct start script (Render uses this by default):

```
// package.json
"scripts": {
    "start": "node server.js", // Ensure this starts your server
    "test": "..."
},
```

4. Commit and push these changes to your Git repository.

Deployment Steps on Render (General Flow):

1. **Sign Up/Log In:** Create an account on Render.com.
2. **New Web Service:** From your dashboard, click "New +" and select "Web Service".

3. **Connect Repository:** Connect your GitHub/GitLab/Bitbucket account and select the repository containing your Express application.
4. **Configure Service:**
   - **Name:** Give your service a unique name (e.g., `my-express-tasks-app`).
   - **Region:** Choose a server region close to your users.
   - **Branch:** Select the branch to deploy (e.g., `main` or `master`).
   - **Root Directory:** Leave blank if `package.json` is in the root, otherwise specify the subdirectory.
   - **Runtime:** Select "Node". Render usually detects this.
   - **Build Command:** Render typically defaults to `npm install`. You usually don't need to change this unless you have a separate build step (e.g., for TypeScript).
   - **Start Command:** Render defaults to `npm start`. Ensure this matches your `package.json` script to run `node server.js`.
   - **Plan:** Select the plan (e.g., "Free" tier for starting out).
5. **Add Environment Variables:** Click "Advanced", then go to the "Environment Variables" section. This is crucial! Add variables for:
   - `NODE_ENV: production`
   - `MONGODB_URI`: Your *production* database connection string (consider using Render's managed database service or another provider like MongoDB Atlas).
   - `SESSION_SECRET`: A strong, random secret for session signing.
   - Any other API keys or secrets your application needs. **Never commit secrets directly to your Git repository.**
6. **Create Web Service:** Click the "Create Web Service" button.
7. **Deployment:** Render will automatically pull your code, run the build command (`npm install`), and then run the start command (`npm start`). You can watch the deployment logs.
8. **Access:** Once deployed, Render provides you with a public URL (e.g., `https://my-express-tasks-app.onrender.com`) where your application is live!

Subsequent pushes to the specified branch in your repository will typically trigger automatic redeployments on Render.

VPS Deployment Concepts

If you choose the VPS path, you'll need to perform several setup tasks yourself. Here's a conceptual overview:

1. **Server Setup:**

   - Provision a VPS from a provider (DigitalOcean, Linode, AWS EC2, etc.). Choose an operating system (Ubuntu LTS is common).
   - Connect via SSH.
   - Perform initial security hardening: create a non-root user with `sudo` privileges, set up a firewall (like `ufw`), configure SSH key authentication (disabling password login).
   - Install Node.js and npm (using a version manager like `nvm` is highly recommended to easily switch Node versions).
   - Install Git: `sudo apt update && sudo apt install git` (on Ubuntu/Debian).
   - Install your database (e.g., MongoDB, PostgreSQL) or configure access to a remote/managed database.

2. **Get Code onto Server:**

   - `git clone` your repository onto the server.
   - Use `git pull` for subsequent updates.

3. **Install Dependencies:**

   - Navigate to your application directory.
   - Run `npm install --production` to install only the necessary production dependencies.

4. **Set Environment Variables:**

   - Set the required environment variables (`NODE_ENV`, `PORT`, `DATABASE_URI`, `SESSION_SECRET`, etc.). You can do this by exporting them in the user's profile (`~/.bashrc`, `~/.profile`), using systemd service files, or using `.env` files managed by a process manager (though be cautious with permissions).

5. **Process Manager (PM2):** Running `node server.js` directly in the terminal is not suitable for production. If you close the terminal or the app crashes, it stops. A process manager keeps your Node.js application running reliably. PM2 is a very popular choice.

   - **Install:** `sudo npm install pm2 -g` (install globally).
   - **Start:** `pm2 start server.js --name my-app` (start the app and give it a name).
   - **Manage:**
     - `pm2 list`: Show running processes.
     - `pm2 logs my-app`: View logs for your app.

- pm2 stop my-app, pm2 restart my-app, pm2 delete my-app.
    - pm2 save: Save the current process list.
    - pm2 startup: Generate a command to run on server boot to automatically restart your saved PM2 processes.
6. **Reverse Proxy (Nginx):** While your Node app runs (e.g., on port 3000), you typically don't expose that port directly to the internet. A web server like Nginx acts as a reverse proxy:

- **Listens:** On standard ports 80 (HTTP) and 443 (HTTPS).
- **Forwards:** Routes incoming requests to your Node application running locally (e.g., http://localhost:3000).
- **Benefits:** Can handle SSL/TLS termination (HTTPS), serve static files very efficiently (often faster than Node), perform load balancing, enable caching, and provide an additional security layer.
- **Install:** sudo apt install nginx.
- **Configure:** Create a server block configuration file in /etc/nginx/sites-available/, defining how to handle requests for your domain and proxy them to your Node app using proxy_pass http://localhost:3000;. Enable the site by creating a symbolic link in /etc/nginx/sites-enabled/ and restart Nginx (sudo systemctl restart nginx).
- **HTTPS:** Use Certbot (sudo apt install certbot python3-certbot-nginx) with the Nginx plugin to easily obtain and configure free Let's Encrypt SSL certificates (sudo certbot --nginx -d yourdomain.com).

This VPS setup provides maximum control but requires ongoing maintenance and system administration effort.

Continuous Integration / Continuous Deployment (CI/CD)

Manually deploying (even with PaaS) after every change can become repetitive and error-prone. **CI/CD** aims to automate this process.

- **Continuous Integration (CI):** Automatically building and testing your code every time changes are pushed to a repository (e.g., running npm install and npm test).
- **Continuous Deployment (CD):** Automatically deploying the application to production (or staging) *if* the CI steps (build and test) pass successfully.

Benefits:

- Faster feedback on code changes.
- Reduced risk of manual deployment errors.
- Ensures tests are always run before deployment.
- More consistent and frequent releases.

Tools:

- **GitHub Actions:** Integrated CI/CD service within GitHub.
- **GitLab CI/CD:** Integrated CI/CD service within GitLab.
- **Jenkins:** A popular open-source automation server.
- **CircleCI, Travis CI:** Cloud-based CI/CD services.

A typical simple workflow defined in a configuration file (e.g., `.github/workflows/main.yml` for GitHub Actions):

1. **Trigger:** On push to the `main` branch.
2. **Job:** Set up Node.js environment.
3. **Steps:**
   - Checkout code.
   - Install dependencies (`npm ci` - often preferred in CI for faster, reliable installs using `package-lock.json`).
   - Run tests (`npm test`).
   - If tests pass, deploy (using CLI tools for your PaaS provider, SSH scripts for VPS, or Docker commands).

Setting up CI/CD pipelines streamlines your development workflow significantly once configured.

Chapter Summary

Deployment marks the exciting transition from development to making your application accessible online. In this chapter, we stressed the importance of preparing for production by setting `NODE_ENV=production`, managing configuration via environment variables, implementing robust logging, and ensuring user-friendly error handling.

We explored the primary deployment strategies: Platform as a Service (PaaS) for ease of use and managed infrastructure (like Render or Heroku), Infrastructure as a Service (IaaS/VPS) for full control but requiring server management (DigitalOcean, Linode, AWS EC2), and containerization (Docker/Kubernetes) for advanced scalability and consistency. You walked through a practical example of deploying to a PaaS provider (Render) and learned the essential concepts for VPS deployment, including server setup, using a process manager like **PM2** to keep your app running, and setting up a reverse proxy like **Nginx** for handling traffic and SSL. Finally, we introduced the concept of **CI/CD** for automating the build, test, and deployment pipeline using tools like GitHub Actions.

Choosing the right deployment strategy depends on your project's needs, scale, budget, and your team's expertise. With your tested, secure, and now deployable application, you've completed the core journey of this book! The final chapter will offer pointers on where to go next to continue expanding your Node.js and Express development skills.

Chapter 14: Where to Go Next

Congratulations! You've journeyed through the core concepts of building web applications and APIs using Node.js and Express. From understanding Node's event-driven nature and handling HTTP requests, through harnessing the power of Express for routing and middleware, managing data with databases and Mongoose, handling user input and sessions, securing your application, testing your code, and finally deploying it to the world – you've built a solid foundation.

This book aimed to give you the essential tools and understanding to get started and build functional applications. But the world of web development is vast and constantly evolving. Node.js and its ecosystem offer countless avenues for further exploration and specialization. Consider this chapter not an end, but a signpost pointing towards exciting new paths you can take to deepen your knowledge and build even more sophisticated applications.

Advanced Express Concepts

While we covered the fundamentals, Express has more nuances and advanced patterns:

- **Advanced Middleware Patterns:** Explore creating more complex middleware for tasks like caching responses, fine-grained authorization (role-based access control), data transformation pipelines, or integrating with third-party services. Look into error handling patterns beyond a single catch-all handler.
- **Streams:** Node.js heavily utilizes streams for efficient handling of large amounts of data (like file uploads/downloads or processing large datasets) without loading everything into memory. Learn how to work with readable, writable, and transform streams within your Express applications for better

performance and memory management, especially when dealing with file I/O or large API responses.

- **Performance Optimization:** Investigate techniques for profiling your Express application to identify bottlenecks. Learn about caching strategies (in-memory, Redis), optimizing database queries, using asynchronous operations effectively, and configuring Node.js clustering to utilize multiple CPU cores.
- **Dependency Injection:** For very large applications, explore patterns like Dependency Injection to manage how different components (controllers, services, repositories) get their dependencies, improving testability and decoupling.

Frontend Frameworks

Our focus has been primarily on the backend. However, most modern web applications have rich, interactive user interfaces built with client-side JavaScript frameworks. Your Express API (Chapter 10) is perfectly positioned to serve data to these frameworks:

- **React:** A popular library for building user interfaces with a component-based architecture.
- **Vue.js:** Another progressive framework known for its approachability and flexibility.
- **Angular:** A comprehensive platform and framework for building large-scale applications.
- **Svelte:** A newer approach that compiles your code into highly efficient imperative JavaScript at build time.

Learning one of these frameworks will allow you to build Single Page Applications (SPAs) or dynamic frontends that communicate with your Express backend via the RESTful API you learned to create.

Real-time Communication

HTTP is primarily a request-response protocol. What if you need instantaneous, two-way communication between the server and clients? Think of chat applications, live notifications, collaborative editing tools, or real-time dashboards.

- **WebSockets:** A protocol providing full-duplex communication channels over a single TCP connection. Libraries like `socket.io` build upon WebSockets, providing easier APIs, fallback mechanisms, and features like broadcasting messages to multiple clients. Integrating `socket.io` with your Express application opens up possibilities for building real-time features.

Different Data Stores

We focused on MongoDB with Mongoose. Broaden your horizons by exploring other data storage solutions:

- **SQL Databases:** Dive deeper into relational databases like **PostgreSQL** or **MySQL**. Learn SQL query language fundamentals, understand relational database design principles (normalization), and explore Node.js libraries (ORMs like Sequelize or TypeORM, or lower-level drivers) for interacting with them. Understanding both SQL and NoSQL gives you greater flexibility in choosing the right tool for the job.
- **Caching with Redis:** Learn about **Redis**, an incredibly fast in-memory key-value store. It's commonly used for caching frequently accessed database query results, storing session data (as an alternative session store), or implementing rate limiting, significantly improving application performance.

TypeScript with Node/Express

As applications grow in size and complexity, JavaScript's dynamic typing can sometimes lead to runtime errors that are harder to catch during development. **TypeScript** is a superset of JavaScript that adds static typing.

- **Benefits:** Catch type-related errors at compile time (before running the code), improved code readability and maintainability, better tooling (autocompletion, refactoring), easier collaboration on large projects.
- **Integration:** TypeScript integrates smoothly with Node.js and Express. You write your code in `.ts` files, and the TypeScript compiler (`tsc`) transpiles it into standard JavaScript that Node.js can execute. Type definitions for Express and most popular libraries are readily available. Learning TypeScript can make your larger Node.js projects more robust.

GraphQL

REST (Chapter 10) is the dominant style for APIs, but **GraphQL** offers an alternative approach, particularly well-suited for complex data requirements and evolving APIs.

- **Concept:** GraphQL is a query language for your API. Instead of multiple endpoints for different resources (/users, /tasks), you typically have a single endpoint. Clients send queries specifying *exactly* the data fields they need, and the server responds with only that data.

- **Benefits:** Prevents over-fetching (getting more data than needed) and under-fetching (having to make multiple requests to get all related data), provides strong typing via a schema, enables API evolution without versioning in the same way as REST.
- **Integration:** Libraries like `graphql.js` and `apollo-server-express` allow you to build GraphQL APIs alongside or instead of REST APIs in your Express application.

Serverless Architectures

While we deployed our application to traditional servers (or PaaS which manages servers), **serverless** computing offers another model.

- **Concept:** You write application logic as individual functions (e.g., AWS Lambda, Google Cloud Functions, Azure Functions). These functions run in response to events (like an HTTP request via an API Gateway, a database update, or a file upload). The cloud provider automatically manages the underlying infrastructure, scaling, and execution.
- **Benefits:** Automatic scaling, pay-per-execution (potentially cost-effective for variable workloads), reduced operational overhead.
- **Use with Express:** While seemingly different, you can often run Express applications within serverless functions using adapter libraries (like `server-less-http` or `aws-serverless-express`), allowing you to leverage the Express framework in a serverless environment, especially for API routes.

Contributing to Open Source

The Node.js and Express ecosystem thrives on open-source contributions. As you become more proficient, consider giving back:

- **Reporting Bugs:** Find issues in libraries you use? Report them clearly on their GitHub repository.
- **Improving Documentation:** Good documentation is invaluable. Suggest clarifications or add examples.
- **Fixing Bugs:** Find a bug you can fix? Submit a pull request!
- **Developing New Features:** Contribute new functionality to your favorite libraries.

Contributing to open source is a fantastic way to learn, improve your skills, build your network, and help the community that provides these powerful tools.

Keep Learning and Building!

The most important step is to **keep practicing**. Build your own projects, experiment with different libraries and techniques, read blog posts, follow tutorials, and engage with the vibrant Node.js community. The journey of learning web development is continuous, but with the foundation you've built throughout this book, you're well-equipped to tackle new challenges and create amazing things with Node.js and Express.

Thank you for joining me on this exploration. I hope you feel empowered and excited to continue building on the web!